SESSIONS WITH ESTHER

Smyth & Helwys Publishing, Inc.
6316 Peake Road
Macon, Georgia 31210-3960
1-800-747-3016
© 2020 by Charles Qualls

Library of Congress Cataloging-in-Publication Data

Names: Qualls, Charles, author.
Title: Sessions with Esther : compelling stories and cautionary tales / by
   Charles Qualls.
Description: Macon, GA : Smyth & Helwys Publishing, 2020. | Includes
   bibliographical references. | Summary: "Sessions with Esther is a
   ten-session study unit designed to provide a compelling look at the book
   of Esther. Each session is followed by a a page of questions that allow
   for a deeper experience of the scriptural passages"-- Provided by
   publisher.
Identifiers: LCCN 2020045974 (print) | LCCN 2020045975 (ebook) | ISBN
   9781641732840 (paperback) | ISBN 9781641732857 (ebook)
Subjects: LCSH: Bible. Esther--Textbooks.
Classification: LCC BS1375.55 .Q35 2020 (print) | LCC BS1375.55 (ebook) |
   DDC 222/.906--dc23
LC record available at https://lccn.loc.gov/2020045974
LC ebook record available at https://lccn.loc.gov/2020045975

Disclaimer of Liability: With respect to statements of opinion or fact available in this work of nonfiction, Smyth & Helwys Publishing Inc. nor any of its employees, makes any warranty, express or implied, or assumes any legal liability or responsibility for the accuracy or completeness of any information disclosed, or represents that its use would not infringe privately-owned rights.

Sessions *with* Esther

● ● ● *Compelling* Stories and *Cautionary* Tales

Charles Qualls

SMYTH&HELWYS
PUBLISHING, INCORPORATED — MACON, GEORGIA

Also by Charles Qualls

Building Blocks for Sunday School Growth
(with Bo Prosser and Michael D. McCullar)

Divorce Ministry: A Guidebook

A Hungry Soul Desperate to Taste God's Grace
Honest Prayers for Life

Lessons from the Cloth
501 One-minute Motivators for Leaders (with Bo Prosser)

Lessons from the Cloth
501 More One-minute Motivators for Leaders (with Bo Prosser)

Marriage Ministry: A Guidebook (with Bo Prosser)

Sessions with John and Jude
God's Abiding Words for an Active Faith

Sessions with Judges
Colorful Characters and Powerful Tales

Dedication

To all the strong, capable, and gifted women God has called, for a moment such as this, or for any other moment in history.

Especially to all the colleagues I have had in ministry who happened to be female. You have inspired and encouraged me. You have taught and challenged me.

The churches I have served have also been led by strong and capable women. Gladys Chancey and Ruby Werts at Milledgeville, Lois Edinger at Greensboro, Melody Mulaik and Judy Burge at Second-Ponce in Atlanta and Peggy Morgan at Franklin are emblematic of some of the great lay leaders I have had the pleasure to work with.

We simply would not be where we are in faith or life without you. We all, men and women, owe you far more than we understand. None more so than the gifted woman with whom I share life, Elizabeth.

Contents

Introducing Esther. 1

Session 1: Vashti's Stand and the Political Realities
at Work 11
Esther 1:1–2:18

Session 2: Mordecai Listens and Haman Schemes 21
Esther 2:19–3:15

Session 3: Esther's Dilemma and Mordecai's Challenge . . 29
Esther 4:1-17

Session 4: Esther Prepares Her Audience 39
Esther 5:1-8

Session 5: Mordecai's Offense 49
Esther 5:9-14

Session 6: Bet You Didn't See That Coming 57
Esther 6:1-14

Session 7: Esther Exposes Haman 67
Esther 7:1-10

Session 8: Esther and Mordecai Are Rewarded 77
Esther 8:1-8

Session 9: Rescue of the Jews 85
Esther 8:9-17

Session 10: Establishment of Purim and Aftermath 93
Esther 9–10

Works Cited 103

Introducing Esther

I love a good story. I have always felt that an interesting tale was worth the investment of time, both by the teller and the listener. I was raised in the Deep South. Storytelling, whether in written form or in oral tradition, is woven into the culture. No matter if you're attending a fall festival, a family reunion, or a funeral visitation, someone is probably off to the side telling a story. Our Bible is packed with surprising, well-developed tales that are skillfully told. Some are longer while others are quite compact.

For whatever reason, when a person walks up to a group of people listening to another person tell a story, the newcomer often feels the need to announce themselves. Maybe the intention is to greet everyone rather than wait for a break in the tale. Perhaps unintentionally, this person interrupts whatever is being said. Often they squelch a good story that was just reaching its conclusion, causing it to wither on the vine.

My wife has come to know that if I am the one telling a story, people had better get ready for me to reconvene the interrupted group and finish what I started. She can almost quote my mantra about this situation. I will usually say, "I'm going to finish this up because I believe that no good story ought to be left behind." Esther is a story you are going to want to pursue all the way to the finish.

No doubt, you know the qualities of an enjoyable story. The telling needs a clever unfolding that might take a while. In the hands of a skilled writer or teller, a story may have details that sound extraneous at the time. In the end, though, they all turn out to have been part of the support structure. Sometimes foreshadowing is there, right in front of us, but cleverly disguised enough that we can only spot it in retrospect.

Harper Lee's *To Kill a Mockingbird* comes to mind. In the first two paragraphs of the novel, Lee gives the reader the story's ending—all of it in one little summary. But the reader has no way to know about this spoiler. The reader thinks Lee is simply starting at the beginning and that these details will be important to know sooner rather than later. Instead, Lee goes on to unfold the story more conventionally until at last we come full circuit. She tells her tale skillfully.

Esther is a compelling, well-told biblical story. Esther's bravery and conviction are instructional. So are her cousin Mordecai's vision and steadiness. We can learn from them as characters. We ought to fight off distractions as we read and make our way to the finish. A good story can cause us to ask important questions about life and self. Our perspectives of certain characters may change as the story unfolds.

In the book of Esther, Queen Vashti emerges early with a pretentiousness that makes her at least interesting. But look again. Why is she so uninterested in what many would assume to be a fairytale existence? Is she simply weary of being queen to an apparently drunken and clueless king?

Haman is the obvious villain, easy to dislike. He is the empowered underling who, left unchecked, eventually over-functions in his role. He abuses his power, seeks status, revels in his riches, and plots the demise of an entire people. Seemingly on a personal grudge, he determines that genocide is a reasonable move.

King Ahasuerus is a cautionary figure, readily showing what can happen when someone with great power shirks responsibility. The king appears to reside happily and perpetually asleep at the controls. Thankfully, Mordecai and Esther are on the job and can be used by God for a good outcome.

That is the overview of the book. Now I advise you to take Esther one study session at a time. Resist rushing to the end. Dialogue with the characters you meet. Interview them and hold them accountable in the ways that strike you. Let yourself ask the questions that are appropriate when reading Scripture, and be sure to learn any attendant lessons that greet you along the way. Enjoy the study, but work at it as much as you can.

Why Study Esther?

I tend to labor under an old-school notion that Esther is a biblical book and therefore has great value automatically. Similarly, I also tend to hold that all biblical books are sacred and have spiritual value for us. Some are more interesting to a broader audience, and some are less so. Certainly, as the book of Esther unfolds and some of its central themes come to light, there are riches awaiting us. We'll explore those themes a little later in this introduction.

Despite my confidence in the value of biblical books, there have been some debates over whether Esther should have been included in the biblical canon. Central to that difference of opinions is that God's name is never directly or overtly used in the book. That aspect alone makes this a unique Bible study series. Be careful about letting it become an obstacle, though. Open yourself to how we might hear from, behold, and learn from a God who might not be named. In the book of Esther, God is present and at work all the same.

Women, in particular, lift up Esther as a worthy read because of how she stands as a positive biblical role model. Sadly, the patriarchal culture of the biblical eras left us far too few Esthers to study. We can marvel here at how prominently her bravery and conviction are featured.

Queen Vashti appears briefly, and we do well to dig for a little background as we struggle to understand her part of the story. In the first session, we'll examine how she may have arisen to her status as queen against her will. Her courageous refusal to play along with her drunken husband's request at a party is bold. What would cause her to take that stand? We should recognize her story as emblematic of how relatively powerless a woman can be in the Bible. Vashti pays a high price for seizing what little power she has. Perhaps she is a strong role model in her own right.

Esther's story will inspire and challenge us to do more and to be better people. We might read this story and wonder what in our lives needs more boldness, more wisdom, more patience, or more action from us. An inspired reader might finish a biblical book like this and believe or live differently as a result.

Esther's story should caution us as well—not just about the people around us and not just about structures and systems, as their complexity can sometimes be lost on us until seemingly too late. Some of the challenge of Esther may be that we see how easily we could become one of the cautionary characters in the story. How easily might I lose my moral compass like Haman did? What crucial element might I not be paying attention to, the way King Ahasuerus missed what was happening around him?

The inspiration we should draw from key characters is also awaiting us in these studies. Mordecai demonstrates wisdom and judgment that should encourage us. How can I be more like him? Esther herself takes action in a crowning moment, demonstrating strength and a dedication to values. For instance, Esther clings to the practice of her faith as she carries out her strategy. Also, she will not just save her own life, but will hold out for a plan that saves her entire ethnic group. Her people inspire her to do more than she might have ever thought possible. Maybe, in turn, she will inspire us.

Central Themes

While the biblical book of Esther reads as one large story that unfolds slowly, important themes emerge early. My hope is that you will be an active student and not a passive one as you journey through Esther. An active student should ask questions of the biblical text.

Why? is always a good question to ask of a biblical story. That question is not disrespectful or doubting. Instead, asking "why?" may lead you to some unusual places. At other times it will yield spiritual riches that will grow your faith. Questions of all varieties will deepen your study: *How did this experience affect the character? What should I learn from it? Why is studying this story valuable for my life of faith?* Naturally, active study like this will lead you to discover your own lessons and notice different themes that may emerge.

You will draw some of your own conclusions as you study. I encourage you to use the inside covers or blank pages of this book for your study notes. Jot your questions and reactions that come up as you read. Be sure to listen to your inner voice for key themes that help this story come alive. Here are some central themes that spoke to me:

• *An empowered woman lives into her purpose at a critical moment.* Lest we have too casual a notion about Esther's bravery, we'll find out that her actions were not without great personal risk.
• *An over-functioning and ambitious underling abuses his power.* Was Haman such a bad person? Maybe he was. Did he slowly become intoxicated by his own power and by the supreme power he spent so much time near? Maybe he simply lost perspective about what was "bad" versus what was okay to do. Maybe he was pure evil. You'll have to decide as you read.

- *A neglectful leader endangers his people.* Do you ever talk to the characters in a story, a book, a television show, or a movie? During a frightening thriller, I'll ask, "Now, why did you go and do that?" as a character makes an obviously bad decision that will likely cost them. We call out, "Look over your shoulder!" to the horror movie character who fails to sense a looming threat. We say, "Don't trust him!" to a character who is a little too naive at the moment. Keep an eye on King Ahasuerus. There is so much he should have known and done, but he didn't.
- *The Jewish people narrowly avoid genocide.* When a Jewish person tells you that their people group has withstood more instances than they can count where someone wanted to wipe them out, believe them. Here is yet another such incident, played out in the pages of Esther.
- *The Bible contains violence and inhumanity.* Some don't study certain biblical stories because they are uncomfortable engaging with issues such as slavery, violence, and genocide. This book is one of those. If we throw out all the stories that feature murder, deceit, violence, and genocide, we are left with a Bible that is easier to read—but at what cost? I urge you to push through. Struggle. Reckon. But keep the stories, all of them. Learn from them, even the cautionary and disturbing ones.
- *The surprising power of deceit is on display in Esther.* We can fool others, and we can fool ourselves. But being deceitful requires great amounts of energy and time from us. Watch the deceit at work in Esther—both overt and subtle. Even Esther's brave plot to save her people involves some deceit.
- *Irony or the idea of reversal is sprinkled into Esther's story.* At times in these sessions, you will see ironies or reversals discussed as "turns." Will the powerful always be the most powerful? Will the least regarded eventually have their day? How fast will the mighty fall? How can some people talk so often but say so little? On the other hand, how can the quietest people end up saying so much when the moment is right? To what extent might the riskiest option pay off in the biggest way? When can violence be used against its own creator? Look for the irony, the reversals, the turns in Esther's story.

Who Wrote Esther?

In Carol Bechtel's volume on Esther, she says the first question that confronts scholars is "Which book of Esther?" Or said another way, the question is, "Whose book of Esther?" The Masoretic Text (or MT) is a Hebrew version of Esther, from which our English translations are typically generated. Jews and Protestants tend to use that one. However, Bechtel notes that Eastern Orthodox and Roman Catholic Christians seem to more widely use a version that is reliant on the Greek Septuagint (or LXX). Importantly, the LXX Esther contains six sections the MT Esther does not have (Bechtel, 1–4). Protestants long ago took the LXX additions to Esther and moved them into the Apocryphal collection—that is, the scriptural readings that did not get voted into the biblical canon but provide meaningful or insightful material.

Esther's true origin is hard to establish. Scholars believe that Esther is a stellar example of a biblical story that was passed along orally for quite some time before someone finally wrote it down. The easy or short answer to authorship is that no one knows who wrote Esther's story.

There are just enough whispers of Mordecai as the perpetuator of Esther's story that the idea warrants mentioning. Esther's cousin Mordecai, who is himself a major player in the story, could have written it down, but no one can substantiate that limited tradition. Some Palestinian Jew, perhaps not even from the area of Susa, seems to have heard and eventually recorded this powerful story so that it would be preserved or could be disseminated.

When Was Esther Written?

Bernhard W. Anderson notes that not a single "pre-Christian" writer refers specifically to Esther, and the book is not quoted once in the New Testament Scriptures. He says that the first evidence of the book was in the LXX (Septuagint) version (Anderson, 827–28). The Septuagint, or "70," was a collection of Greek translations of the ancient Hebrew texts. One legend held that seventy-two translators, six each from all twelve tribes of Israel, were sent to Alexandria to work on the publication because of the growing number of Jews living in Egypt by that time. The Torah seems to have been translated first, completed by at least the mid-third century BCE. The rest of the translation was completed perhaps by the middle of the second century BCE.

Anderson says that Josephus quotes from the LXX Esther and counts Esther among twenty-two books that had long been held sacred. Sadly, nothing from within the book of Esther speaks to identify its own time period, though the story appears to be set during the late Persian period (538–333 BCE). Scholars do see chronological and cultural missteps within Esther that indicate its author lived later than the period of time portrayed. For instance, the Dispersion seems to have happened before Esther was written and is a part of the writer's backdrop.

Maybe the Maccabean revolution is the right time period. The character Haman wishes to extinguish all the Jews in the area. That matches up with the wishes of Antiochus IV, who wanted to cleanse the land and restock it with good and less troublesome Hellenists, so some scholars look to a brief restoration of the culture after the Judas Maccabaeus revolt (165–135 BCE) as a possible time placement for this story.

Others see an absence of allusions to Jerusalem, or even to Palestine, as troublesome for a Maccabean timetable. The people of that era seemed to be fighting for their survival as Jews as well as for their individual lives. Since they were not an autonomous people, they also seemed to be trying to win over someone else's leaders to value them as human beings. For instance, in Esther we will see the empire's second in command give an order that would annihilate all Jews. They might not have seemed to be human to him, if he were willing to do this simply on a grudge against one Jewish person. If this seems too early for the Maccabean period, then perhaps the time of the Dispersion itself (later Persian, 350–330 BCE) is more accurate. No one knows for certain.

What Is Esther's Place within the Biblical Canon?

As alluded to earlier, God is not mentioned overtly in the book of Esther. Yahweh is never named, credited, or mentioned as particularly moving among the characters. No other names for God appear in the book either. That omission of God, once noticed, can be troubling for some readers.

Martin Luther, for instance, had a list of biblical books that he disapproved of in the canon. Esther was among these, according to some accounts. His issues with these books appear to be at least twofold. If Luther found a biblical book lacking in theological content or depth, he questioned its fit in the biblical canon. Likewise, a biblical book that elevated the status or position of Jews too highly also violated his convictions. Esther seems to commit both sins in his view. Luther found Esther to be an "honorable" book but not a fitting one to include as sacred and holy Scripture.

A curious thing happens, though, for others who read Esther. These readers might not always catch on to God's overt absence because mention of "the Jews" is so prevalent. The net effect is that many readers unwittingly have the notion that this is the story of God's people. The biblical association of Jews with God creates an outcome opposite to Luther's conclusion. It may well be the best way to read Esther.

In an earlier section, we noted some of the themes that arise in Esther's story. Those may be the beginning place for discussing Esther's role in Scripture. Her story illuminates the themes in a vivid, inspiring way. For that, Esther is important to us. Her story also demonstrates, once again, how fragile a place the Jews have occupied in their history as a people. The intended mass harm to them that serves as the story's central plot takes its place in the larger history of this important ethnic and spiritual group. Consider the toll the biblical antecedents of Christ would have paid if Haman's plan on the gallows had been allowed to unfold.

Esther can also caution us against a few institutional realities. Power unchecked can quickly become power misused. Esther shows us what can happen when an unavailable or uninterested leader loosens control in favor of someone with little or no moorings. The powerlessness that many people in our culture live with is also on display in Esther. There are too few players who seem able to do anything about the events going terribly wrong. As we read, we know some things that need to happen in the story. However, no one seems to have a legitimate opportunity to do those things. What if Esther herself had not acted boldly?

Women particularly seem to love Esther today, and for reasons we should note. The Bible portrays a patriarchal life. The history and cultures shown, as well as the times and settings, explain this even if they do not satisfactorily resolve it for us. Church history since biblical times has given us little that is different. Many Western churches have tended to rely heavily on the talents, efforts, and willingness of women while steadfastly recognizing men as the primary leaders.

Anecdotally, many Christians who have lived even in these last 150 years might read our own published church histories and see a different reality. If it weren't for the women who have served, taught, led, and taken risks, then many of us wouldn't have local churches today. Instinctively, we know that especially the church's recent Western history does not match up with the ancient patriarchal tones we accept as biblical.

Here, then, is Esther, whose story shows her taking a risky and bold step at the end. Esther is both convictional and practical. She calculates her costs and balances them against the needs of her people. With nothing solid to depend on, she extends herself in a vulnerable way. Her courage not only wins the day but also serves as an inspiring model for women and men in a genre where there are all too few women represented.

Finally, the Jewish festival of Purim is centrally tied to this story. Like Hanukkah, Purim celebrates Jewish deliverance and is held in high esteem as a ritual observance to be strictly kept. In contrast to Hanukkah, though, the deliverance commemorated in Purim is not so much about liberty as about Jewish preservation. Therefore, Purim is a joyful celebration to be embraced.

This group of Jewish people living in Persia is scheduled for annihilation, according to Esther's story. From the brink of disaster, they are not only spared but valued. During Purim celebrations, amid all the eating, drinking, and laughing, there is also a reading of the book of Esther. Anderson says that some rabbis go as far as to declare that even if all the words of the prophets were to be lost, Esther must always be remembered and Purim always observed (Anderson, 828–32). In one of our sessions, we will study the part of the book in which the festival of Purim is established.

Session 1

Vashti's Stand and the Political Realities at Work

Focal text: Esther 1:1–2:18

"Let's Begin at the Beginning . . ."

"Let's begin at the beginning" is a popular way to express the start of something that may become a bit complicated later. Across history, women have had to take principled stands to break the strangling grasp of patriarchy. Some of these women are well known for their stances, but others are less so.

One pastor tells of the time in 1972 when his mother argued with a car dealer until she was red-faced and almost canceled the deal. She had a job working outside the home, the car was to be her vehicle, and she wanted her name on the title. The car dealer insisted that her husband's name must be listed instead. Nowadays, that likely would not happen. Back then, it was locally groundbreaking for her to hold the title to the car.

Anne Hutchinson paid a steep price of banishment from her New England colony in 1638, which led indirectly to her death out in the wilderness—because she dared to confront the male ministers in her area. They were teaching what she saw as a "works-based" theology while discounting a more "grace-grounded" approach. Hutchinson was banned from living within the settlement. Similarly, the Quaker Mary Dyer was hanged in colonial Boston for practicing her banned expression of faith. Addie Davis was a Baptist who took a principled stand, and, in 1964, became the first woman to be ordained as a Southern Baptist pastor.

In 2012, fifteen-year-old Pakistani student Malala Yousafzai was shot for her public stance that young women in her country ought to have equal rights to education. The Taliban had at times stopped young women from going to school. A gunman stopped her bus, boarded it, and called out, "Which one of you is Malala?" When she answered, he fired. She survived her attack and emerged as a worldwide advocate for human rights. She was awarded the 2014 Nobel Prize for her courageous and convicted stance.

The patriarchal backdrop becomes so normal in our Bibles that many of us have been raised to read it without notice of the inequities. In John 8, our sacred Scripture tells the story of Jesus talking with a woman who was apparently caught committing adultery all alone, for no man is accused of the same crime alongside her. Jesus saves her from being stoned for "her" crime. We take the title of Matthew 14's "Feeding of the Five Thousand" at face value, even though verse 21 indicates that there were far more, but the women and children were not counted. These are but two examples of the ways the patriarchal structures affected women in the Bible.

Who Was Vashti?

At the beginning of the book of Esther, Vashti, the disenchanted queen, takes a principled stand by refusing to submit to her husband's summons. It is a prelude to Esther's similar stand, though on a first read we may not realize the connection. While Vashti is not one of the better-known characters in the Old Testament, many women have admired her courage as a model of strength when the odds are stacked against her. She is an unempowered voice who speaks out anyway.

Despite the few verses in Esther dedicated to Vashti, her independence has resonated with writers. Harriet Beecher Stowe once referred to Vashti's rebellion here in Esther as "the first stand for women's rights" (Stowe, 197). There is a chapter in Charlotte Brontë's novel *Villette* titled "Vashti," which describes Lucy Snowe's reaction to a powerful actress she calls Vashti, whose performance "disclosed power like a deep, swollen winter river" (300). James Weldon Johnson's poem simply titled "Vashti" imagines the speaker as the beautiful queen's lowly servant who meets her again years after her banishment.

While this book of the Bible shows Esther carrying what seems to be the vast share of the load, we begin with Queen Vashti's brave stand. Some readers might wonder, "What was so bad about Vashti's life? Why would she rebel when it looks like she had it made?" If we read her story with the assumption that being chosen by a king to be his queen is equal to winning some kind of fairytale lottery, then these are our natural questions.

Modern readers might envision the happy endings of Disney's *Beauty and the Beast* and other princess movies. In them, love reigns happily ever after. Much dancing and singing ensue, and romance is in the air as the story ends. However, to understand Vashti's world in Esther, we need to focus on a different part of the Beauty and the Beast story. We should look at the beginning, where Belle is forced to live in an enchanted castle against her will. She longs to return home and yearns for her simple life in a small village among family, friends, and all her books. Time passes, and this young woman, who appears to have every luxury life can offer, is a miserable captive instead. The female characters in other Disney movies have similar circumstances—held captive in a certain way of life and longing to break free. It seems that this is what life was like for Queen Vashti.

One Party after Another

If you have read Esther 1:1–2:18, you might think the book is about lavish parties. These verses mention three of them, and we read great detail of the themes and the people who are invited. One of the parties is finally spoiled by Queen Vashti's refusal to be presented for display before the king and his attendees. The lavish show of wealth and power by King Ahasuerus of Persia is conspicuous.

W. S. McCullough, in his article titled "Ahasuerus," points out that there is some disagreement in ancient Scripture texts as to the identity of Esther's king. While the MT scripts of Esther identify him as we do here, "Ahasuerus," the LXX identifies him as "Xerxes." Ahasuerus appears not only in Esther but also in Ezra 4:6 and Daniel 9:1. Meanwhile, many scholars believe the latter identity (Xerxes) fits better with the story's Persian setting. This would place his reign from 486–465 BCE. If that is the case, he would have been the son of the Old Testament king Darius and the father of Artaxerxes, who ruled later.

History and the biblical story cannot be completely in agreement on this, for each possibility carries details that match and other details that do not. The ancient Persian Empire was centered in what we know today as Iran. For our purposes, what is important here is the bitter displacement suffered by Vashti and her people. She was an exile living within a new setting in Ahasuerus's vast empire. His holdings stretched from parts of Asia to Africa, including modern-day Ethiopia and Sudan. His wealth and power are obvious.

As we study this session's text, we note the imbalance within the story. The biblical text lets out a long leash for Ahasuerus to show off what he has. The story labors to tell about his extravagant parties. We get it. He is the king. Finally, Vashti, whom we do not really get to know, does two quick things. Esther 1:9 says that she gives her own party for a group of women. Then, she commits her act of rebellion when summoned by the king. His immediate reaction is to replace her.

As Bible students, we can almost get whiplash trying to process how a bunch of happy parties went wrong so quickly. Let's unpack the sordid details. It is the seventh day of a long party. A vastly drunken king sends his seven eunuchs to fetch his presumably beautiful queen. He wants to show her off to his friends.

The trouble is, Vashti is in no mood to play along. We never hear her say a word. Nor do we get an explanation of why she refused his instruction to appear. Why might the queen have caused all this trouble? If you have ever reached a point in a relationship, in an organization, or within a company where you simply no longer cared what happened to you, then you might relate to Vashti.

Since Esther's biblical book was written, rabbis have argued over Vashti's image in this story. Some are sympathetic to her, while others cast her as yet another spoiled villain. As students of the Bible, we'll have to draw our own conclusions. Let's look at some different components of the story. First, the king interrupts Vashti's own party with his presumptuous order. We are reminded that he is in power, not Vashti. All that she has is his. Her life is never truly hers.

Second, the Jewish commentary called the *Midrash* might come the closest of any document to explaining Vashti's attitude. There, Vashti is identified as the great-granddaughter of King Nebuchadnezzar II of Babylon and the daughter of King Belshazzar. Her great-grandfather had once sacked Jerusalem in conquering the southern kingdom for Babylon. Thus, some Jewish historians view Vashti as a villain herself. A group of Medes and Persians later invaded a great portion of Babylon and took it for the Persian Empire, killing much of her family. Effectively, King Darius of Persia is said to have "given" Vashti to his son, Ahasuerus, as a wife.

In this context, we have a more complete picture of a displaced woman living in grief over her loss of place and family. She is forced to assume the title of queen as her husband assumes the throne, living under a reign she never wanted. Vashti is a hostage being summoned by a drunken king who appears to care for her far more because of her beauty than because of any real or grounded love.

Additionally, much has been made of the king's orders that night. In Esther 1:10-11, Vashti's summons includes the following detail: she is to stand "before the king, wearing the royal crown, in order to show the peoples and the officials her beauty; for she was fair to behold." Some rabbis and scholars think this means she was supposed to be naked, wearing *only* her crown. If that is so, it is even easier to understand how the king has finally pushed her too far.

Years of captivity, living within a lavish prison, might have finally caught up with Vashti. Only a shallow reading could leave one to suppose that her wealth-by-association, or royal status by marriage, would be enough to supplant her underlying grief or frustration. It appears that she has lost any caution about the real danger she could face. Something propels her to place her life on the line and refuse the king's order.

As a preview to the political intrigue that is to follow, Esther 1:12–2:4 reveals the layers of the king's reaction: from feeling fury, to listening to the sages and officials, to displacing Vashti, to the issuing of decrees and sending letters. His minions have missed no chance to point out that Vashti's disobedience will make him look weak when the story is told far and wide, so he acts to secure the patriarchal structure. He decrees "all women will give honor to their husbands, high and low alike" (v. 20), and sends letters declaring "every man should be master in his own house" (v. 22).

Soon, a new search is announced, for the position of queen is now open. In the remainder of our session text, Esther 2:5-18, we read about the elaborate campaign to find a new queen.

Lather, Rinse, and Repeat

Finally, briefly, we meet Esther. Let's take in the biographical details we get here. She is another displaced captive within the vast Persian Empire. Her family has been spirited away by King Nebuchadnezzar of Babylon, and an apparently beautiful Esther is now placed in "custody" (2:8) as a contestant in the search for Ahasuerus's new queen. Her wait during the twelve-month rite ("six months with oil of myrrh and six months with perfumes and cosmetics," 2:12) of purification is striking. Finally, all of the qualified virgins can be paraded in front of the king. It is as though Vashti's story is now repeating itself in Esther's.

This story will test our biblical comfort, as even a cursory reading makes it apparent that each virgin is ultimately required to spend a night with the king. Each one is to bring a gift to present to

King Ahasuerus. Then, if he enjoys himself enough, the candidate for queen will graduate to a new harem as one of his concubines. Esther finds favor with Hegai, the eunuch in charge of the king's virgins. We gather that she is given inside information on what item or gift she can take that will most please the king.

Our text ends with Esther winning the position as queen. The king's lavish celebration begins, with tax benefits extended into all provinces. Another great party is thrown. The crown is placed on Esther's head, and with it comes the heaviness that will culminate several chapters later as her circumstances only grow worse.

There is a sense of déjà vu as Vashti's time as queen gives way to Esther's. However, pushing past that obvious layer, we cannot help but notice the patriarchal roots of the Bible's place and time. Women displaced with their families are treated as property to be given and taken. The men have all the power while the women have almost none, aside from the power they are willing to exert at great personal risk. Two women have become queen now, seemingly neither due to love but instead due to their outward beauty. We live in an age and culture where this should cause us to recoil. Now the stage is set for the patient unfolding of the book of Esther's drama.

1. What woman in history stands out to you because she acted on her own sense of empowerment?

_____
_____
_____
_____
_____

2. What difference did she make as a result of the action you admire?

_____
_____
_____
_____
_____

3. As you began this study, what did you already know about Esther, either the biblical book or the woman herself?

_____
_____
_____
_____
_____

4. Why might Vashti have been a hurting and frustrated queen even before the king ordered her to come to his party?

_____
_____
_____
_____
_____

5. What might be some reasons that Vashti finally took a stand?

6. In one sentence, how might you summarize why this first chapter suddenly pivots from happy parties to a rebellious queen in trouble?

7. After reading two chapters in Esther, how would you describe King Ahasuerus?

8. How do the apparent roles, as portrayed here so far, compare with your assumptions about normal relationships between kings and queens?

9. How do queens seem to get chosen in Esther's story?

_____
_____
_____
_____
_____

10. In what ways do you work to manage your reactions to the patriarchal culture of biblical times? Why is the study of Scripture worth our patience with those problematic dimensions?

_____
_____
_____
_____
_____

Session 2

Mordecai Listens and Haman Schemes

Focal text: Esther 2:19–3:15

Right Place, Right Time

We can learn a lot just by listening. The evidence comes to us from all quarters of life. In a class to work toward my college management minor, one professor taught a brief unit on "Management by Wandering Around." His contention was that in addition to the structured activities that might involve meetings, communication, study, and projections, part of good management was getting out and wandering around a bit—listening, observing, and learning from the inside of the organization (Peters and Waterman).

In the Revolutionary War, General George Washington is said to have made brilliant use of spies. These observers were well disguised because his network was made up of regular, everyday people. They had been recruited to gather and pass along information learned as they came in contact with British leaders. Time after time, Washington received early and helpful information. Likewise, in World War II, Allied forces developed sophisticated means of decoding Nazi and Japanese communications so that they could make more informed strategy decisions.

Not all good listening is done by managers or military leaders. We all have a chance to use our ears and our eyes to know more of what is going on around us. I once worked with a leader who taught me that I could "split" my hearing. That is, he said, one could listen to a primary conversation while simultaneously overhearing a nearby discussion. At first, I thought he was putting me on. Then, I began to try this myself and realized he was right. Television news anchors do something similar all the time, delivering their scripts while simultaneously listening to a producer's cues in their earpieces.

Sometimes, in the course of being observant, we may even overhear things we wish we hadn't. Many know the sting of walking up to conversation in which a friend or loved one is being spoken of unflatteringly. In an age of social media, people we love or respect may post things that make us think less of them. Sometimes, bad or surprising news that we did not seek out comes our way. We wish we could unhear what we know, but we cannot.

Earlier in Esther 2 (v. 15), we learned that Esther was the daughter of Abihail, Mordecai's uncle. She and Mordecai were cousins although we get the notion that she was young enough that he adopted her as though she were his own child and helped raise her.

In Esther 2:19, we read that Mordecai is in the gate area of the city. The wording in the text is unclear if read only in English translations. What unfolds may sound as though it happens before a new queen is chosen. Instead, the original Hebrew indicates that there was a second gathering of virgins for a ceremonial or other purpose that the English text does not make clear.

As Esther begins her reign as queen, Mordecai picks up on a plot to assassinate King Ahasuerus. The writer of Esther gives us a clear and important detail here in verse 20. Esther, at Mordecai's counsel, had not yet revealed who her people were; that is, she had told no one that she was of Hebrew descent. However, Mordecai had not taken his own advice and evidently had spoken at work of his ancestry.

Some Bible interpreters believe that perhaps his placement in a job at the king's gate was a protective measure since a guard detail was already established there. This would assume that the king at least knew that his new queen was related to Mordecai (Bechtel, 34). So the possibility is that Mordecai, as Esther's closest relative, was given a position of some responsibility. However, later in the book, Esther 8:1 implies that Esther did not tell King Ahasuerus about her relationship to Mordecai until after Haman fell from grace and was punished with death. If we take the chronology in Esther at face value, then, Mordecai earned a position of responsibility at the gate by his own merit.

Either way, Mordecai is depicted as being in the right place at the right time. While he sits there, some disgruntled eunuchs plot to assassinate the king, and Mordecai overhears them. We are not told why they wanted their ruler murdered. Esther 2:21 does tell us that these two guards watched over the king's apartment entrance, so they had close, daily access to the king. Something they saw or heard made them terribly upset with him (Anderson, 846).

The timing of the story indicates that this incident took place early in Esther's role as queen. Mordecai did what seemed most prudent and told Esther of the imminent danger. Esther went straight to the king with the news of an assassination plot and credited Mordecai for discovering and reporting the plan.

Verse 23 demonstrates that the king took his new queen seriously and launched an investigation. Evidence apparently lent credence to the story. The plotters were hanged on the gallows, and the event was recorded in the empire's own book of chronicles. Only important events were so recorded. There is no mention of any immediate reward for Mordecai, however.

Previous Bad Blood?

Haman's promotion as the king's nearest and most trusted assistant in 3:1-2 is striking in light of Mordecai's loyalty. Seemingly without reward, Mordecai again fades to the background, and out of nowhere, the character named Haman is at the center of our story.

Why wasn't Mordecai given such a trusted position in the aftermath of proving his loyalty? We cannot fully answer this question. Perhaps he had not otherwise distinguished himself and was still relatively unknown to Ahasuerus. We know from our own work and other settings that sometimes a person from within our ranks rises and serves brilliantly in a critical moment, yet we also know that they will never reach the top level of leadership no matter how grateful we are for their momentary contribution.

At the 1996 Atlanta Olympics, a security guard named Richard Jewell had a heroic moment. Up to that time, he'd had a checkered past in law enforcement. He had taken the one job he could get working with the games. Jewell became a national hero when he spotted a suspicious backpack sitting near a media tower. He managed to alert authorities and begin forming a safe perimeter. Though there were severe injuries when terrorist Eric Rudolph's bomb exploded in that bag, Jewell's attentiveness and action kept it from being far worse. In the aftermath, Jewell was falsely implicated as a suspect. Once his name was cleared, though, he settled back into his accustomed role. For the rest of his life, he drifted from one job to another in small, rural law enforcement agencies.

Bernard Anderson, in his exegesis of Esther, sheds interesting light on what happens next with a suddenly empowered Haman.

Anderson contends that there was a lingering tension between Haman's people and the members of Mordecai's ancestral tribe, the Benjaminites. Anderson cites the historian Josephus, who interpreted Haman's title "the Agagite" as meaning that he was an "Amalekite." During the reign of King Saul, there was mention of one Amalekite king named Agog (1 Sam 15:8). It is likely that Haman was a descendant of King Agog. Anderson says that this interpretation is also found in the Talmud (Anderson, 847).

Anderson describes an apparently bitter and sometimes violent "blood feud" between the Benjaminites and the Amalekites. This dissension may lie in the background of the tension between Haman and Mordecai in Esther. In 3:1-2, we read that Haman is now set above all the princes who were with Ahasuerus. The king has issued a decree illustrating how powerful Haman is, commanding that all the people are to bow down to Haman.

Mordecai's refusal to bow is noted and viewed as a disobedient affront. Partial though we may be to Mordecai, he was still expected to be subservient in his role under Haman. When asked why he will not bow, or give "obeisance," to Haman, Mordecai is depicted as merely responding that he is "a Jew" (v. 4). This refusal is, of course, not acceptable in a Persian courtesan practice. What he may have meant was that he claimed an ethnic or spiritual superiority to Haman. We are not clearly told why Mordecai rebelled.

Too Much Too Soon?

Sometimes we say "the punishment does not fit the crime." Therapists and leaders alike occasionally classify a reaction as "disproportionate to the offense." For whatever reason, Haman declines to punish Mordecai. However, he is perfectly willing to plot the genocide of the Jews within the empire—all of Mordecai's ethnic group. Esther 3:5-15 shows the revenge forming and then being enacted.

When have you observed someone being handed too much power too soon? Within politics, companies, churches, and other organizations, we see this happen occasionally. Even children are supposed to be taught that there is a difference between what we may legally do versus what we *should* do. There is supposed to be a moral or ethical set of filters that helps guide us in making such judgments.

But sometimes these filters are ignored. The new CEO is given the controls and shocks the company's culture by implementing immediate personnel changes and practices that are within his power but not within good judgment. The baseball coach takes last year's star pitcher, a closer, and inexplicably demotes him to middle relief. The new pastor is told that she must work with the existing ministerial staff she inherits. Rather than fire anyone, she begins to target and slight some of them until they appear to leave voluntarily.

Haman apparently lacks good judgment. Certainly, he seems devoid of basic human decency. In this part of our text, we see him misuse the power he has been given to develop an elaborate network of resources. All Jews within the vast empire are to be rounded up and prepared for execution. He even runs this new action plan past the king, who sleepily waves his hand and approves of whatever Haman thinks is best. Ahasuerus grants Haman the funding to carry out his plan. Haman is given too much power too soon.

A good book chapter may end with a plot-driven cliffhanger. A television show will often edit toward a commercial break by creating tension with a mystery or a question that viewers will want to see solved or answered. They will have to come back after the break. Even movies often use a "tease" after the end credits to create an unresolved situation so that the audience simply must come back and see it addressed in the sequel. As our session text ends with 3:15, Haman's plot is fully developed. The people of the capital city, Susa, are perplexed by what they hear: a day is coming when all Jews are to be murdered. With this cliffhanger, we can't help wanting to come back for more.

What should we do with what we have already studied in Esther? Do we need to know how things are going to end so we can draw lessons from what we have already read? There are some life themes and pertinent plot lines in today's text that may prove instructive:

• Haman's overly ambitious streak makes him a cautionary figure for us all.

• The king probably gives too much of his power to an underling who is not ready for such resources and possibilities.

• Haman's overreaction to feeling threatened by Mordecai (for whatever reason) should hold up a mirror to us. We can injure others simply by acting out on unresolved past issues, slights, or hurts we carry.

• Mordecai did something responsible with the information he overheard. Esther acted on that same information in a timely and right way. We should be challenged by their determination and bravery.

1. What is the most vivid "right-place, right-time" story from your own life? What happened because of that serendipity?

2. What are the best ways that listening helps you to grow in your faith?

3. How do you make decisions about what to do with sensitive information?

4. What kind of reward should Mordecai have received for his loyalty in reporting the assassination plot? Should he have been promoted? Why or why not?

5. What do you recall about the battles and skirmishes the ancient Israelites had with other people groups in the Old Testament? Why might Haman, an Amalekite, and Mordecai, a Jew, have animosity toward each other?

_____
_____
_____
_____
_____

6. When your faith is pitted against a request, a law, or a custom, how do you evaluate whether to comply or to resist?

_____
_____
_____
_____
_____

7. Who or what has stood out to you as a real-life example of "too much power too soon"?

_____
_____
_____
_____
_____

8. What are some helpful guidelines when deciding whether a punishment fits or exceeds the offense?

_____
_____
_____
_____
_____

9. Why would Haman be willing to commit genocide and kill all the Jews?

_____
_____
_____
_____
_____

10. What are lessons we can take away from this session in Esther? What questions do you wish it had answered? Why does it matter that we have studied this scriptural text from Esther?

_____
_____
_____
_____
_____

Esther's Dilemma and Mordecai's Challenge

Session 3

Focal text: Esther 4:1-17

The Strain of Fear or Disappointment

As I write, the Covid-19 pandemic still spreads across our world. By the time you read this, perhaps the constant headlines will have yielded to stories of recovery, but now, the pandemic is still a cautionary medical tale with geopolitical implications, and too many have suffered or lost their lives. Those faces of family, friends, and neighbors are making the pandemic all too real. May we never forget.

A beloved entertainer has succumbed to the ravages of this illness. Nationally known politicians have been diagnosed with positive test results. Closer to home, a hospital nearly across the street from our house has lost its first diagnosed patient with this deadly new strain of the coronavirus. Some of you who read this will have lost a loved one to the virus. There are other faces, though. Leaders who stepped up to the moment. Medical professionals and first responders who, at personal risk, treated those in need while managing their own sense of being overwhelmed.

People deal with fear and disappointment differently. Some take these journeys inward, while others act out more openly. Sometimes the source of someone's behavior is obvious because the facts of their situation are known. Word gets around, usually, about a severe illness, death, or tragedy that they have faced. Other times, though, the motivation behind a person's outward actions or words is a secret buried within.

In Esther 4:1, Mordecai grieves the decree that King Ahasuerus has set in place. Within the empire, all of Mordecai's people, the Jews, are scheduled for elimination. They will be rounded up in every province and simultaneously executed at a date soon to come.

The king not only has permitted Haman to arrange this genocide but also has granted the funding to make it happen.

We recoil, wondering why human life was not valued more highly in the ancient world. Stories like the one in Esther or tales of humans used in violent "games" at Rome's ancient colosseum confuse us. Then again, we must consider history. We move forward in the centuries and read about the conquests, oppressions, and injustices that were every bit as culturally entrenched as they were in Esther's story.

Then we consider our own time and the discriminatory or unjust social, political, and economic practices in which we may participate. Like other societies around the globe, we elect the people who create or sustain these policies, and then we wonder why human life is not valued more highly.

As we read Esther 4:1-3, we might admit that we do not understand Mordecai's way of grieving. We read about the ancient Hebrew practice of "sackcloth and ashes" at various points in Scripture. In Genesis 37:34, Jacob tears his clothing, puts on sackcloth, and mourns his son. In 2 Samuel 3:31, the anointed David declares a time of sackcloth and mourning at the death of Abner. In Psalm 30:11, the writer rejoices because God has ended his grief. His sackcloth has been removed and he has instead been clothed with joy. When Job finishes his epic dialogue with God and sees the limitations of his own wisdom and perspective, he repents. In Job 42:1-6, he expresses himself to Yahweh and says that he sits in ashes. In Jonah 3, the king of Nineveh calls for national repentance, and he tears his clothes off to sit in ashes while wearing sackcloth or burlap.

Cultures around the world, and regions within some nations, have a variety of ways to express grief. Some people are quiet and observe periods of isolation. Others have large gatherings and rituals. Still others may be loud and demonstrative in their sadness, leaving others around them who do not understand to wonder about the outpouring of emotion.

"Sackcloth" was a type of cloth normally made from goat's hair. Some biblical translations render the word "burlap," but the two cloths seem to be a bit different. There is no specific shape or cut indicated in the Old Testament, so much has been left to our conjecture. This could have been a single garment or, at times, layers of garments (Jacobs and Nowack).

What were the layers of Mordecai's deep grieving? We can speculate as fellow human beings, even if we live in a different place and time. Any person would likely have some degree of personal concern when facing such a decree. Mordecai himself was set to die now. His own mortality was placed starkly in front of him because of someone else's power to end his life. Mordecai's loved ones would also suffer along with him. No doubt, his thoughts were of family and friends alike. Then, the powerful tradition of Hebrew peoplehood compels us to remember that at least within this empire, any Jews under Haman's control would be wiped out in one massive destruction. That loss of culture, history, and ethnic identity would be heavy to consider.

At first, Esther has no idea why Mordecai is wearing sackcloth, making himself ineligible to pass into the area of the king's gate. She must be unaware of the decree, living inside the palace in a sheltered existence. In 4:4-9, she sends a eunuch to inquire as to why her relative is so emotional and demonstrative. Mordecai tells the eunuch everything that has happened and even sends a copy of the decree back to Esther.

The Right Word of Challenge from the Right Person

Again, we notice that King Ahasuerus holds the ultimate power in his court. Esther's reaction to the murderous decree is immediate and practical. She knows that she cannot simply go into where the king is and express her concerns.

Apparently, a month has passed since Esther has been invited even to be near the king (v. 11). This detail piques our curiosity and confusion; Esther has not seen the king lately, and she is subject to the same death penalty as anyone else in the empire if she takes it upon herself to approach him. She is a "queen" in title, with little if any real power. Her relationship with him, up to this point, seems to exist only at his behest.

Life is complicated, and opposing ideas can be true at the same time. When we crave a particular outcome to a situation, we sometimes oversimplify the details. No doubt, Esther might have been just as horrified as Mordecai once she heard about the death sentence for their people. Still, her situation was complicated. At first blush, all she could sense was that she had no choice in the matter.

Mordecai likely knew of the issues she faced, yet he also seemed to see things that were as yet still far ahead. He conjectured that Queen Esther, if she were discovered to be a Jew, might not be spared the death edict (v. 13). We are not likely to ever know whether he was correct from a legal standpoint since the Persian Empire now lives mostly in the legends of antiquity. Esther sent her reply, and Mordecai neither wasted time nor minced words in his response, as we read in Esther 4:10-14.

This brings us to another opportunity to learn from Esther and Mordecai. We may catch ourselves saying, "But I have no choice." Esther seems to have said this to Mordecai. However, upon a further look at a complicated situation, we may realize we have a choice or even two. It may be that we don't like the options, but they are at least options. Esther had a choice in front of her—just not a very palatable one. None of us would have liked the implications of the choice Mordecai was asking her to make.

How many times have you or someone you respect in the faith recited Esther 4:14b? "Who knows? Perhaps you have come to royal dignity for just such a time as this." We usually remove mention of "royal dignity" and fill in the blank with the new job, the promotion, or the serendipitous circumstances of the moment. I had someone say to me just the other day, "Who knows? Maybe you have become pastor of the church for just such a time as this." We try to encourage or challenge someone to rise to the demands of a given moment. Plucked out of context, this part of the verse is inspirational. I have attended events whose chosen slogan read "For Such a Time as This."

As much as we like that notion, we might wince as we hear Mordecai's challenge in Esther 4:10-14. We feel empathy for her. Asked perhaps to sacrifice her life on the chance that the king might sympathize and overrule Haman's action, Esther is being put in a perilous, complicated position. When someone else's life is at stake, we call on them to do something brave. When our own life is at stake, though, the situation appears more complicated.

Here is where we need to work out a problem. If you are studying with a group, you might ask them, "What is the difference between *bravery* and *recklessness*?" If you are reading this book and studying independently, you might pose this question to a friend over coffee or to your family over dinner. This is a key issue at our present juncture in Esther's story.

Military service people during a war or terrorism threat are looked on as bravely serving their country. First responders are consistently regarded in this way because their job requires them to run toward gunfire, a car wreck, or flames. During the current Covid-19 pandemic, medical personnel such as doctors and nurses are especially heralded for their bravery. They work long hours while risking their personal health to battle the dangerous virus and try to save lives.

Mordecai's challenge to Esther would have required extreme fortitude from her that some might call "bravery." This is one of the reasons that Esther inspires so many people. This woman of relatively little power used the one convenient office she held, that of a token queen, to save an entire people.

What one person might call "brave," however, another might call "reckless." They might consider that there is more to live for than this one moment. There could be a family at home, a bright or otherwise long future ahead, or maybe other people who rely on that individual. These can be compelling arguments for why someone's service might be at least as equally reckless as it is brave. When it's your life, I will be inspired and call you brave. When it's my own life, your favorite option for what I should do could start to look a little reckless.

Who is the one person to speak the deepest truth into your life? Who is the one person to best tell you the things you don't want to hear? Who is the most likely to inspire you to do things for them that you might not do for others? Mordecai may have been the one person who had any right to ask such a sacrifice of Esther.

He made a prudent point; she might be killed anyway if her identity as a Jew were known. The palace might offer little safety, seeing as how disposable queens appeared to be in Ahasuerus's court. Apparently, though, Mordecai convinced Esther that her brave action would be her people's only chance. They desperately needed her to take it. She may have, in turn, been one of the few who could persuade the sleepy king to wake up and avert a tragedy for her people.

We do not know specifically what Mordecai refers to in verse 14 when he says that Esther and her father's family will perish if she doesn't go to the king. His challenge alleges that God will punish Esther if she fails to act. Because God isn't mentioned, Mordecai seems to make an aspirational faith statement here without us getting to know what grounded it.

Misery Loves Company

Can you hear Esther saying, "Oh, all right"? Worn down perhaps by the urgency of the moment or by the fact that her dear Mordecai makes the plea, Esther decides to take the risk. Now she has her own request.

In return for her willingness to act, Esther wants support (v. 16). This is akin to the church member facing serious surgery. Rather than keeping it a secret, they entrust their faith community with the news and invite them to join in prayerful support. We like to know that we are not alone. The higher the stakes, the more we feel the need for supporters to be on board with us.

Look what Esther asks Mordecai to do, beginning with verse 16: "Go, gather all the Jews to be found in Susa, and hold a fast on my behalf, and neither eat nor drink for three days, night or day. I and my maids will also fast as you do. After that I will go to the king, though it is against the law; and if I perish, I perish."

I don't want to underestimate the spiritual transaction Esther might value here. We cannot know to what degree her request reflects the ancient practices of her faith tradition. Prayer and fasting were hallmarks of the Hebrews, especially when they were waiting for God to act or even when they were reacting to how God had acted. Esther may want to be sure everything possible is done to prepare her to take this opportunity and speak with the king.

As for her final note, I have heard words like that before: "If I perish, I perish." At a previous church, one of my members needed a drastic and long surgery to address an abdominal aneurysm. At that time, the mortality rate for her specific surgery was about 80 percent. Yet if the problem went unaddressed, her mortality prediction was 100 percent. I tend to hear Esther's words in that same spirit. She is not flippantly addressing her chance of dying, but she also understands that she and her people have no choice other than the dangerous option. The other outcome is even worse.

We can hear resignation in her words. She has committed to the fate that awaits her. She has no control over how the king will react. Possibly, she has found some reason to trust that the king will give her a fair hearing. We can only imagine that. Overall, she has weighed the variables and decided that her people matter more to her now than even her own life. All she asks is that those very people support her.

Fulfilling Esther's request for prayer and fasting may also endanger Mordecai. Although there is likely a Hebrew underground network, if he is discovered as the organizer of this spiritual fast, he might suffer. Mordecai puts skin in the game, so to speak, beyond the threat of Haman's royal decree. Mordecai and the Jewish people are being asked to take a risk along with Esther. Passing along

Esther's request carries a great risk for him. Both are reacting to their situation in ways that are anything but passive.

Thus ends today's study, and unless we have read to the end we still do not know how this situation will work out. Can you appreciate the cliffhanger that sets up the next session? Don't you wish you could have been an onlooker to hear how these exchanges between Esther and Mordecai sounded? No doubt, the king's chambers will be a fascinating place for Esther to find herself asking for his favor. We will see what happens in session 4.

1. What are your assumptions about the value of human life in the ancient world compared with its value in our world today?

2. When you hear about some of the "games" in the ancient world, where humans were killed for sport while an audience watched, how do you react?

3. What are some examples of abuse, genocide, or poor treatment of humans within the Bible?

4. In our time, what are some examples that stand out to you in which human life or human worth is not highly valued?

5. How do you deal with fear or disappointment? Do you tend to keep those feelings inside, or do you tend to act outwardly on your strong feelings?

_____
_____
_____
_____
_____

6. What is the difference between *bravery* and *recklessness*?

_____
_____
_____
_____
_____

7. Who is one person who can speak deep truth into your life? Why do they get this privilege, perhaps above other people in your circle of influence?

_____
_____
_____
_____
_____

8. What are some factors that have caused you to act more boldly than you normally would?

_____
_____
_____
_____
_____

9. What are the risks inherent with what Mordecai asks Esther to do in our story? What are the potential rewards?

_____
_____
_____
_____
_____

10. How does your own faith help you as you process perplexing and difficult decisions?

_____
_____
_____
_____
_____

Session 4

Esther Prepares Her Audience

Focal text: Esther 5:1-8

What's Legal vs. What's Right

When I was a child, Christmas Eve at our house was a magical night. As many children do, we wondered if Santa would come to visit while we were sleeping. The next morning was always filled with surprises. We rarely ever got what we had asked for, but what we got was almost always just as good if not better.

One year, my older brother involved me in his latest Christmas-related scheme. Our parents knew we would have trouble sleeping that night because we were simply too excited. That was true each Christmas Eve. So they let us stay in one room together to pass the time if we couldn't sleep. Once our parents were out of earshot, my brother said, "They told us if we needed to visit the bathroom, that was okay. But we are not supposed to pass the bathroom." Just down the hallway from the bathroom was the entry to our living room. Any Christmas surprises in there would be spoiled if we got that far.

He went on to explain an idea based completely in legalism. He was also generous enough to let me try this out first. In retrospect, I realize he did this in case anyone else was still awake. Then I, not him, would be the one caught. His notion was that if I hooked my foot on the entry corner to the bathroom and then leaned far enough forward to see into the living room, I technically would not have passed the bathroom. And I could peer into the living room to see the gifts and toys.

Of course, I was just eager enough (and dumb enough) to try. I would be happy to take a turn. After all, this plan sounded good to me. I took my brother at his word that I would stay in compliance with the instructions our parents had given us. I did it first, and then he had his turn. Thankfully, neither of us were caught. Only years later as adults did we confess about the years we had spent on Christmas Eve doing a stretching and balancing act while trying to peer at our loot from Santa.

In the early days of the 2020 novel coronavirus pandemic, we had the opportunity to learn many lessons. An aspect of these lessons involved the moral and ethical implications of our decision-making. One story that circulated widely was of a man in Tennessee who had the bright idea of cornering the market on bottles of hand sanitizer. He bought 17,700 bottles of the gel. His plan was to sell it all online at inflated prices.

The two largest online sales platforms he attempted to use both shut down his accounts because of the obvious price-gouging. He was soon mostly stuck with his entire inventory, with no practical way to get rid of it. Arguments ensued as people reacted to the story. One camp suggested that this was simply good old American capitalism at work—supply and demand in action. The other side insisted that he and others like him were taking advantage of people in need in a protracted, desperate time. Neither side argued that what he had done was illegal. His stockpile and plan were within legal bounds. Yet he was wrong. This was a moral wrong wrapped in a legal scheme. (Once his story was published in the *New York Times* and Tennessee's attorney general began an investigation, the man donated the hand sanitizer to people in need across Tennessee and Kentucky.)

Esther's Plan

As Esther 4 ends, Mordecai has made a compelling case to Esther that she is uniquely postured to save her people. In return, Esther has asked Mordecai to rally the Hebrews and have them join with her, praying and fasting for three days and nights. Now, in chapter 5, the time for action has come.

Esther needed a good plan if she had any hope of making an appeal to the king. The law was not on her side. Haman's horrible plot to kill the Jews was completely legal within Ahasuerus's court law. The king was also personally protected by laws that restricted who could approach him. Esther would have to work within legal bounds, ironically trying to thwart a completely legal problem.

A constant theme in this study has been the absolute power King Ahasuerus held over everyone around him. He handed over stewardship of that power largely to Haman, but there was no mistaking that at any moment the uninterested king could awaken and decide to do whatever he wanted.

Still, he was not the only one with power. We should remember that in a working relationship, power can be granted by office or position. Ahasuerus's power was absolute, and it came with the office he held. But power can also be earned and granted. He had granted Haman considerable influence within the kingdom. Esther also begin to exert her own power. Her power, though, is subtler. Her influence will have to be earned by her cunning and her willingness to act.

Carol Bechtel (51) points out an important transition that becomes evident in chapter 5. Our story here not only tells us what happens next. It also shows us that Esther is now stepping into her role as queen. To the extent that she can, with calculated and measured strength, she is moving forward on her mission to save her people. Her caution is necessary if she is to stay alive long enough to accomplish her mission.

Esther is smart enough not to go walking into the king's court without an invitation. Our study in session 3 made the case that even a queen in the ancient Persian court could not do that. She had to be invited. However, if she used her power wisely, she might be able to bring that invitation about.

Esther is also smart enough to develop a layered strategy. Her goal is to register her concern about the impending demise of the Jewish people and then to influence the king to undo Haman's order before it is too late. She will not simply blurt out her request or report the news of Haman's plan the first time she sees the king. Although the text is silent on the matter, Mordecai may have served as a consultant as she devised the plan.

Since the text has told us straightforwardly that Esther is attractive (2:7), an honest reading of chapter 5 brings her appearance into play. Esther adorns herself with royal robes, and, while looking royal and being attractive are not automatically connected, we sense that Esther got the look just right.

A New Reality

Bechtel believes that a new reality is evident in this chapter. Previously, Esther has only been referred to by her first name. Now in Esther 5, she is referred to for the first time as "Queen Esther." She is coming into her own right in front of us. However, a careful reading of verse 1 reminds us who holds the ultimate power. The king is "royal," with no less than six reminders of his status ("king's palace," "king's hall," "the king," "royal throne," "inside the palace," "entrance of the palace"). That dynamic is not for us to like or dislike. It is simply for us to understand.

"On the third day" reminds us that Esther is connected to her people, the Jews, who have fasted and prayed with her in preparation for this moment. The story will not let us forget her ties to them. She gave Mordecai a request to pass along to their shared people. Apparently, he did so, and now time is being marked by where executing her strategy falls within Esther's plan (Bechtel, 51).

In her comments about Esther 5, Kandy Queen-Sutherland points out the importance of symbolic language. When Esther 1:1 opened, the Hebrew word *wayehi* was translated "Now it happened . . ." as we met King Ahasuerus. Now in 5:1, the same Hebrew word is used. The phrase "Now it happened . . ." is not included in the NRSV translation. However, it is in the ancient manuscripts. Since the king was introduced that way in Esther 1, this phrase marks Esther's movement forward as a stronger player in the story.

Queen-Sutherland also notes certain "groupings" in the text. As we come to know the king and Esther as leaders, specific details are presented in threes. King Ahasuerus is introduced as being in the third year of his reign (Esth 1:3). Soon, three banquets are held (also in Esther 1). Now in chapter 5, Esther begins her assertive action on the third day of her fast with the Jews. Three more banquets will help resolve the story from this point (Queen-Sutherland, 325).

Esther 5:1-2 shows Esther being careful not to enter the king's hall; she enters his court instead and makes sure she is within his line of sight. Her ploy works perfectly, as in verse 2 Ahasuerus extends a golden scepter and invites her to come in. Everyone, it seems, knows his weaknesses and how to play to them. The new queen, Esther, is no exception. Her plan at least lets him think it is his idea to invite her in. Now she has her opening.

Verses 3-5 show Esther ready to answer if the king asks what is on her mind. When he does, Esther has an invitation of her own. "What is it, Queen Esther? What is your request? It shall be given you, even to the half of my kingdom," he says (v. 3). None of us can know how literally to take this part of his response. Would Ahasuerus have really given Esther up to half of his kingdom? Probably not. After all, it seems as if he has already given most of his kingdom away to Haman.

Reidar Bjornard also notes the layers of the queen's savvy. She has been strategic in developing a plan that seems to have hooked the king. Then she has the discipline not simply to rush in and blurt out her question. Now that the king has extended an opening for her to do so, her one request is that he come to dinner. Apparently, she has already set in motion a special banquet for the king and his assistant, Haman, since her invitation is for "today" (v. 4) (Bjornard, 13).

Esther takes more care here than meets the eye. She remembers to invite the king in a manner that postures herself humbly. She also sees to it that the king's assistant is on the guest list. Only in the Hebrew, though, might we catch that she did this in a way that demonstrated Haman was not on the same royal level as the king. In Hebrew, her invitation reads, "If it pleases, let the king come—and Haman—today to the banquet that I have prepared for him." She not only humbles her own position but also flatters the king while being sure that Haman, the lesser of the two men, is included (Bechtel, 52).

We may be excited to see what happens next, but this session's text does not put a closing note on the drama just yet. If we simply want resolution, we're ready to hear Esther make her direct request. If instead we want to learn from Esther, then we should appreciate her discipline. In fact, patience and discipline are hallmarks of how she forms and carries out her plan.

Sometimes we want God to do powerful things for us. Often we wish God would resolve a terrible hardship or move us forward in our lives. What may be required of us is the obedient and measured life of waiting. With her people's gathered life on the line, Esther did not endanger them further by rushing the plan. That is inspiring. It is also instructive if we wish to grow in our faith.

Ecclesiastes 8:11 says, "Because sentence against an evil deed is not executed speedily, the human heart is fully set to do evil." Esther is on a mission to confront evil. Mordecai has left her with little choice. Her conscience and her convicted heart will drive her forward. As is popular to discuss in our age, Esther has to speak truth to power to save her people. But the evil she confronts in Haman has played out within the legal bounds given by the king.

As today's story closes, Haman is put in a position he can't escape. When a king says to his assistant, "Let's go have dinner tonight with the queen," he's not really asking. The assistant can't answer, "Oh, King . . . I have plans." The king's power is absolute. At the banquet Esther gives, she is offered a chance to express her wish, but she simply insists that the two men attend yet another banquet on the following night (v. 8). The king agrees, obligating Haman to come with him yet again.

Everyone in our story is operating in bounds, if strict legalism is our only measure. However, there is tremendous wrong that still needs to be undone. When we misuse the power, resources, and opportunities life gives us, sometimes we pay high prices, even if we have played strictly by all the rules. Esther now has a path to expose Haman's inhuman plot against her people, and she will take it.

1. When have you been tested because something that was legal still did not seem right?

2. How do you find guidance when you are caught up in an issue where the legal choice and the right choice are not the same thing?

3. What is the difference between a moral issue and an ethical one?

4. Think back to a time when you have seen a great plan drawn up and carried out. What were some strategies of pulling off this plan when the odds were not so great?

5. What causes the human heart to sign off on an evil deed, even when the person may know that what they are about to do is wrong?

_____
_____
_____
_____
_____

6. What do you think of Esther's strategy?

_____
_____
_____
_____
_____

7. What do you think you would have done in her situation?

_____
_____
_____
_____
_____

8. What are some lessons we can learn from this session's story?

_____
_____
_____
_____
_____

9. Do Esther's circumstances and her actions remind you of anything in your life or in our world?

_____
_____
_____
_____
_____

10. What are some things in this story that might have been legal but are still wrong?

_____
_____
_____
_____

Session 5: Mordecai's Offense

Focal text: Esther 5:9-14

Our last session ended on a bit of a cliffhanger. Esther had braved approaching the king's court without an invitation. This could have been dangerous for her personally. Though she was well received, it was not yet time to act. First, her plan involved getting the king and his assistant Haman to attend a banquet.

As readers, we want to know how that works out for her. We want to know more. Instead, beginning in verse 9 we get a shift in scenery. Now we are at the king's gate and the banquet has already been held. The current subject is some drama that doesn't involve Esther at all. We will have to wait for her next move.

Not Getting Along

Think of someone with whom you don't seem to get along. Maybe you've never had an actual conflict with them, but, all the same, they get on your nerves. Maybe it's clear that you irritate them. It is not popular to talk about such things among Christians. We are somehow expected to adhere to a code that suggests we have no enemies. It is as though no one should ever annoy us. We act as if it should be easy for us to like everyone—and for everyone to like us.

My mother once said to me, "Honey, in life there will be people who will take one look at you and decide they don't like you. You may never know why. It could be how your nose sits on your face." She probably heard that bit of wisdom from my grandfather. The wording sounds like something he would say. By the way, she was right.

I have found this to be true in life and in ministry. Some people are naturally drawn together from the beginning, while others never find a way to connect. The sound of someone's voice, their facial expressions, or other nonverbal habits may form an unspoken barrier. Just as there is a mystery to what causes two people to "hit it off" instantly, there is a mystery to what keeps some apart.

Haman had a growing dislike of Mordecai. Chapter 5 shows the widening gap between them, and this unfolding subplot seemed important enough for the writer of Esther to interrupt our intrigue with the queen herself so that we can explore it.

Mordecai was stoking the issues by refusing to bow down to Haman (v. 9). To be clear, protocol dictated that he was supposed to bow down any time Haman came along, but Mordecai simply would not. The Scripture does not shed light on what Mordecai disliked about Haman. Clearly, something had happened between the two of them. Or Mordecai refused to acknowledge Haman's authority because of a dynamic we'll probably never understand.

Back in session 3, we explored some reasons for their animosity. There was likely a lingering, generational conflict between Haman's people and Mordecai's ancestors. Tribal issues that caused enmity could have carried forward even to their day. Great power has been conferred upon someone Mordecai already refuses to respect. Perhaps Mordecai thinks this power is too much, too soon for Haman to have earned.

Decades ago, I knew a person who was only a few years older than me. We had overlapped in school. A desperate ladder-climber, he noticeably switched his ideology and his theology in order to position himself to rise within a prevailing new denominational climate. Soon, he landed one of the highest positions in the land. Just after the announcement of his appointment, we had to sit with him at a luncheon. Elizabeth and I discussed later how torturous it was for us to listen as people fawned over him. All the while, we knew what he had done and how disingenuous his image appeared to those of us who knew who he truly was at heart.

Whatever the history of their feud in the book of Esther, Haman's frontline issue is now Mordecai's disrespect. If Mordecai gets away with this insubordination, Haman's power and appearance as a leader will be questioned. Ignoring him is an option, but it's not one Haman cares to try.

Maybe the Money? The Power? The Resistance?

Read aloud Esther 5:9-14. What leaps out at you? Do you find a character here who is in the right while someone else is in the wrong? Do you know enough yet to discern which is which?

Is there anything fundamentally bad or corrupt about a rich person with great power? Is there anything wrong with money? Some Christians talk as though there is. My father worked for a childhood friend who inherited a great fortune as a young adult. I knew the man when I was a child, and I marveled at his riches. However, he cycled through a series of troubled marriages and died quite young with a substance abuse problem.

In his later years, my father's simple observation was that his friend's money had robbed him of his life: "That money ruined him." What my father was expressing referred to several things. The friend felt tremendous pressure from friends and family. He would say, "Everyone in my life wants something from me. No one loves me just for me." He grew cynical and bitter the longer he lived. My dad would make a similar observation about Elvis Presley: "Money and fame killed him."

Do any of these—riches, power, or position—pose a danger to us? Do they render us automatically suspect as individuals? To hear some talk, one might think so. But we do encounter people who adjust to wealth in healthy ways. There are happy rich people who are inspiring with their generosity and kindness. We also find people who can rise to great power, or prominent positions, and use their related resources responsibly.

There are people who are convinced that God hates rich people. They mistake the many biblical stances against injustice and unfair business practices to mean that God is against wealth itself. They gauge the high expectations of those who have riches to mean that God dislikes the rich. Instead, God judges anyone who is not faithful, whether they are rich or poor.

One aspect of this story is the extent to which Haman allows Mordecai to affect how he feels. Verse 9 says that Haman is "happy and in good spirits" as he starts his day. This changes as soon as he sees Mordecai. We are to understand that nothing else has upset him except Mordecai's resistance. How much should what another person thinks, says, or does affect how we feel?

Being Fair to Haman

If we are to understand today's story, we may need to try to be a little fairer to Haman, even if just for a moment. Where I come from, "Bless his heart" is not always insincere. Haman is a key player, the second in charge. His position is right beneath the king himself. Because of his status, people are supposed to bow to Haman. Either by custom or by his own declaration, resistance to this fact is punishable by law. Mordecai gets no say in this matter.

This means that Haman has every right, from a protocol standpoint, to expect people to bow to him if he wishes. *Bless his heart.* That was the system, the rule. You or I may not relate to it or know anyone to whom people are expected to bow. In the United States, we don't even bow to the president. It's not our system. It was Haman's system.

I am probably finished being fair to Haman. We know enough already to sense that Haman is evil. I do not think we are supposed to sympathize with him too much. We can sense the showdown that is coming, where people in the story finally push back against evil. Haman will be the face of that evil.

Kandy Queen-Sutherland poses a helpful comparison between Haman in this story and Boaz in the book of Ruth (333). Both play the "big man" role in their respective books of the Bible. Both have position and power, resources and options. However, there appear to be stark differences in their characters. Queen-Sutherland observes Haman to be "[p]ompous, arrogant, full of himself to the point of incredulity . . . he is the counterpoint to . . . Boaz." Neither man is a king. One of them, Haman, conducts himself as though he is. He is selfish and vindictive. The other, Boaz, has earned his power and wealth in more traditional ways, yet he uses what he has for the good of others. He is easily the more admirable of the two.

When Mordecai refuses to bow to Haman again, here in Esther 5, Haman gives him a pass (v. 10). The text does not explain why. For some reason, Haman chooses not to deal immediately or directly with Mordecai just yet. Instead, he goes home and pulls together a support group.

Now we meet Zeresh, Haman's wife. Together with a close group of friends, Haman embarks on an inner journey presumably to make himself look or feel better. He recounts how much he has achieved, but his actions almost seem out of place at this point.

In verses 10b-11, Haman chronicles his wealth, the number of his sons, and the track of promotions from the king that he has coursed. The fact is, it appears that everything he has is owed to his relationship with the king—except his sons. The number of sons one had was a unit of measure for blessedness or a type of wealth in the Old Testament ancient Hebrew world.

In verse 12, Haman tops everything off by reminding them that he is the only one who has been invited by the queen to attend yet another banquet with the king, to be held the next day. He is important. "Yet all this does me no good so long as I see the Jew Mordecai sitting at the king's gate," he says (v. 13). Haman feels that he is being made to look weak.

Maybe he reveals a part of his bias against Mordecai in what he calls him: "the Jew." This label sounds derogatory here, lending credence to the notion that there was unfinished generational business between his people and Mordecai's. Or Haman simply did not value Jews as real or credible humans. In any event, there is an air of snobbery in his statement.

Anyone can feel better about themselves if they are always surrounded by people who tell them only what they want to hear. Perhaps Haman's friends believed in him and were fully on board with his team. Then again, maybe they had a relationship with him similar to the one he had with King Ahasuerus. That is, perhaps everything they had was due to their being beholden to Haman.

We don't get to know who originated the idea that is suggested. But Zeresh is credited most with voicing or reiterating the suggestion that Haman simply execute Mordecai. The text postures this as a unanimous notion between her and the friends. "Just build a dramatic, prominent gallows and hang him," they suggest. In other words, get rid of Mordecai and make an example of him in the process.

Verse 14 closes with chilling news. This advice to hang Mordecai pleases Haman so much that he orders the gallows to be built. The man truly has a lot of power. To get some perspective on how much of an example would be made of Mordecai, in Genesis 6 Noah's ark is said to have been 30 cubits high. In Exodus 25–27, when God requests that a tabernacle be built for the ark of the covenant, it is only to be built 10 cubits tall.

A cubit was a unit of measure believed to equate to roughly 18–22 inches. Haman's new gallows were to be built to a height of 55 cubits! He and his team were not just going to punish Mordecai; they were going to hang him high. We have forgotten about Esther's delicate plot for a moment. Now we are concerned for Mordecai's future. Will he survive?

1. Think of someone with whom you never seem to get along. Are there reasons for this friction? Is there some mystery to it?

2. Are there things we could learn from a relationship that never seems to go right? What have you learned from the odd relationship you thought of?

3. To this point in our story, what is your understanding—or theory—about why Haman and Mordecai didn't get along?

4. When have you had to "play the game" and get along with someone for the benefit of your career, your family, or your organization?

5. In situations where you are not getting along with a superior or a coworker, by what standards do you judge your options for what you will do?

6. Is there anything fundamentally bad or corrupt about a rich person who has great power?

7. How would you summarize Jesus' attitudes about wealthy or powerful people? How is this substantiated in Scripture?

8. Do any of these—riches, power, or position—pose a danger to us? Do they render anyone automatically suspect as a person?

9. Why might Haman have chosen to kill Mordecai rather than to exercise other options in dealing with their conflict?

_____
_____
_____
_____
_____

10. What does the sheer size of the gallows in the story communicate?

_____
_____
_____
_____
_____

Bet You Didn't See That Coming

Session 6

Focal text: Esther 6:1-14

A curveball. A plot twist. A jaw dropper. A surprising turn of events. Not quite a denouement, though.

Those are some thoughts that might come to mind when you read Esther 6:1-14. Having read this chapter, what do you think? If you are studying with others, that question would be a good starting point: *What do you think about the story we just heard?* Bet you didn't see that coming! I don't think any of us could have envisioned it.

In the Palace

Imagine you are a servant on the night shift. Technically, you are on call, but that doesn't normally mean much because everyone in the royal family is usually asleep. Then whispers start to circulate that the king is restless. He's not finding it easy to sleep on this particular night. The whispers turn to louder confirmations as officers and servants pass each other in the hallways. Someone says, "He wants to hear what?" Another answers, "He wants someone to fetch the book of records and have it read aloud to him. Now!"

In the social media age, a new term has arisen: the *spoiler*. You probably know it well. Here's how it works. Someone has seen a big, feature film at the first showing when it releases. There were surprises in the film that the trailer did not reveal. This person gets on social media and tells it all. Their friends, who also want to see the movie soon, decry them openly because they have now "spoiled" the whole plot. "Gee, thanks for the spoiler!" they reply. Or someone misses the big ballgame because they had to work and doesn't want to hear the final score. They want to watch it later and be surprised. "Please, no spoilers!" they plead.

Well, here's a spoiler alert. There is some business we need to take care of here in order to be responsible Bible students. There is more going on in this text than meets the eye. We could simply read this chapter and take it at face value. There is an insomniac king who needs entertainment. In the process, he stumbles onto an unrecognized hero. "What an eventful night," we could observe.

But that's not good enough. In truth, the whole story of Esther has shifted right in front of us. What happens on the micro level has macro-level implications. Up to now in the book of Esther, King Ahasuerus has been a nearly unnecessary leader, a nonfactor. He's been so lazy that he has delegated all his meaningful power to Haman so that he doesn't have to be bothered with being the king. Ahasuerus only appears interested in the trappings of court life.

I once worked with someone who was incredibly creative. If you needed a party, they could throw it. If you needed a show, they could put it together. If you needed a laugh, they could provide it. But the pastor we both worked with once remarked, "Now if only I could get him to fall in love with the less romantic parts of the job." Like my coworker, King Ahasuerus has no interest in the everyday aspects of his leadership. He loves the banquets, feasts, parties, and attention from servants. He loves court life, including the harem that comes with it. That appears to be about it.

On this restless night, the king is unable to sleep. Here comes the bigger-picture spoiler I told you to expect. This is not just a one-night occurrence. A uninterested, lazy king is about to wake up to what is going on inside his court and outside in his empire. He is about to become alert, and he will finally set things right. In the process, we will witness some terrific irony.

To Ahasuerus's great surprise, he finally hears the story of the man who once foiled the plot hatched by the two disgruntled eunuchs. We finally hear the eunuchs' names, Bigthana and Teresh. From our study of Esther 2 and 3, you may remember that they wished to assassinate the king. Since they worked at the king's gate, these unhappy guards had the access and knowledge to pull off the job—except that Mordecai overheard them plotting and alerted his cousin, the new Queen Esther.

All this time later, the king has finally realized that he should have recognized the unnamed hero. The man who saved his life from the eunuchs' plot is owed a great deal. Can you believe he had not already seen to this honor? That in itself illustrates just how disconnected King Ahasuerus has been.

Word Gets Around

I have spent my ministry career serving larger, rather complex "first church" congregations. First Baptist here and First Baptist there. As such, relative to our settings, we have always had access to leaders and prominent people in the city or community. In some settings, we staff members have been those influential leaders in the area. But I recognized early in my career that there were certain things I could learn or hear only from unexpected sources.

If I wanted to understand some things, the custodian might be the best one to get me up to speed. In one church, we had a cook's assistant who knew some great information. In yet another, there was a longtime administrative assistant who was my institutional historian and town chronicler. She just knew things.

These are not the kinds of people King Ahasuerus talked to. But on this night, when he finally asks them a question, his servants have a ready answer. No one has likely ever asked them. Look at what happens in verse 3. After hearing about Mordecai's heroic act as recorded in the book of records, the king asks, "What honor or distinction has been bestowed on Mordecai for this?" The king's servants who attend him say, "Nothing has been done for him." They knew about this act. No one had to look in the book of records for this answer. No one had to send out for a reply. The insight was right there. The servants who attended to the king knew the answer and gave it to him: "Nothing has been done for him." They had noticed the injustice, the lack of gratitude shown to Mordecai thus far. Word gets around.

Apparently this all-nighter culminates with the king deciding that something must be done to honor Mordecai. We can suppose that because Haman walks into the court just as the king cries out, "Who is in the court?" (v. 4). As chapter 5 ended, Haman had decided he would see the king first thing in the morning to order Mordecai's execution.

Verse 6 is awkward to read, yet it also illustrates how drunk Haman still is on his own stature within the empire. Ahasuerus asks, "What shall be done for the man whom the king wishes to honor?" Haman says to himself, "Whom would the king wish to honor more than me?" Carol Bechtel observes that the humor in this conversation hinges on the fact that we as readers of the text know more than either of the characters do (58–59). The king never bothers to ask what Haman wants in the first place. Haman never bothers to ask questions he should ask, either. They are talking right past each other here.

A lawyer was once working with me on a project that involved filling out forms and then being interviewed. He said to me, "I want to advise you in two ways. First, answer all questions honestly and upfront. But second, don't answer questions they aren't asking yet." His advice was wise. Answer only the essence of the true question, then stop. Next, don't editorialize and risk opening new topics or questions they might not have thought to ask. If Haman weren't so easy to dislike, what happens after this would be harder to read. Instead, we may begin to enjoy the twist that awaits.

Haman starts answering a question that it seems the king has not yet asked him. That is, Haman could have first asked the king whom he wished to honor and maybe even asked a follow-up question inquiring what the person had done. But Haman thinks that he himself must be the honoree. Blinded by his own hubris and ambition, he doesn't consider that he won't be at the center of the king's particular attention. If he had, he might not have been quite so helpful.

Awkward Festivities

In an ironic turn, Haman now unwittingly volunteers a lavish blueprint for Mordecai's festivities. In the process, Haman thwarts his own plan to kill Mordecai. The list is extravagant:
• royal robes that the king has worn
• a horse that the king has ridden
• a royal crown on the horse's head
• the robes and the horse handed to one of the king's most noble officials, who then robes the man whom the king wishes to honor
• the honored man conducted on horseback through the open square of the city, with people proclaiming before him, "Thus shall it be done for the man whom the king wishes to honor" (vv. 8-9).

Apparently, horses often went into battle or into parades with their heads adorned. The more important the person riding the horse, the more ornately their horse might be decorated. Bernhard W. Anderson even documents having seen pictures from a similar time when Assyrian horses were depicted with tall, elaborate head ornaments or "crowns" (859). So this feature of Haman's plan likely was a fitting way to honor someone as important as himself. Or in this case, Mordecai.

Even with Haman being our villain, the next line in verse 10 is painful to read. Because the king likes the plan so much, he directs Haman to carry it out personally. Only now does he reveal the name of the honoree, since Haman has not bothered to ask. The king insists that Haman is not to leave out a single detail he has mentioned, instead carrying out the plan precisely as outlined to honor Mordecai.

We may wonder why the same king who has signed off on Haman's order to eradicate all the Jews within the empire might suddenly decide to honor a Jew. Did he not remember? Did he make an exception for Mordecai? Anderson proposes a theory that is consistent with a king practically asleep at the controls. That is, Ahasuerus might not even have recalled the name of the small people group that Haman had asked permission to wipe out back in Esther 3:1-11 (Anderson, 859).

In fact, we don't know if Haman ever specifically mentioned the word "Jew" to the king back then. If he did, that is not enumerated in the story. What went in the written edict itself might have had the details conveniently hidden from the apathetic king. The king trusted Haman so blindly that he took his ring off, in chapter 3, and handed it to Haman. He gave permission and money for Haman to write the edict and then do as he wished.

It may have mattered so little at the time of the edict that now Mordecai's designation as "the Jew" does not even register with the king. The kingdom at that time would have had a great number of peoples making up its vast holdings. Someone paying scant attention, like this king, may not have kept track of who was who.

Why the Story Matters

Before we move on, let's attend to something important. If you are studying with others, you might discuss: Why should this texture of the story matter to us today? That is, why should this intent to kill the Jews in Esther's story matter to us today?

We come away with some painful layers for reflection. First, we get the impression that in this powerful empire and specifically to these powerful people, human lives appeared disposable. We must place more value on living, breathing people. In the case of Esther's story, an entire people group called the Jews seem to matter little. We must do better.

This brings us to another layer. It is another instance in the long history of the Jewish story where their relatively small size and lack of power left them vulnerable to evil that aspired to wipe them out. No wonder Jews today can easily make the case that they have faced genocide many times.

Finally, consider the value of checks and balances to such great power. No one or two people should have such unbridled power and money. Evil, at a personal or at an institutional level, must be able to be overcome. Civilized societies have checks and balances built in and maintained at the highest governmental levels. But we must value people enough to overcome the worst things that our own rulers might aspire to do on our behalf.

In our story, Haman takes Mordecai on his ride of honor. He proclaims Mordecai's worth through the open square of the city so that all can see. The way the text reads, Haman even voices this announcement himself. Then, he retreats to his home in shame. Grief seems to be more his outward stance (vv. 11-12).

The story ends in a briefly described flurry of important activity. First, Haman's circle of advisers say aloud what he already seems to know. His wife, Zeresh, and the "wise men" foretell that his fall is at hand (v. 13). This is subtle, even sarcastic Hebrew humor used by our story's writer. Those who were called "friends" before as they advised Haman to build tall gallows and hang Mordecai are now referred to as "wise men" in the obvious hindsight of his downfall (Anderson, 860).

Yes, the same crew who put him up to the strategy of having Mordecai executed now pin Haman's downfall on Mordecai's lofty position. Then the eunuchs arrive to whisk Haman off to Esther's banquet (v. 14). In light of what has just happened, and how few options Haman has next, this feels like an ominous ending to the chapter. At the banquet to follow, Haman may get served up on a proverbial platter.

The Fast Swings of Life

Life turns quickly and takes us with it. You will have to decide for yourself whether God controls each victorious and vicious turn life can take. You will have to decide whether God "does" these things to us or not. If God is calling every little shot, then we must work out how a loving God can do so many horrible things to humanity.

Here in Esther, though, we feel solidly that Haman has been a despicable person. Perhaps he has brought pain upon himself on his own terms. There is a biblical notion that we will be judged by the same standards with which we judge. We observe that sometimes we can be hurt by the same means with which we hurt others.

Haman could have handled his rise to power and wealth with more grace. Instead, he reveled in his ability to get away with nearly anything. Haman could have been a loving person rather than a snobby, vengeful one. Haman could have used means to enforce rules and policies other than physical violence and genocide. The expression "a knife that cuts both ways" seems to encapsulate Haman's story. What do you think?

1. What is your reaction to the portion of Esther we are studying today?

2. What book, story, or movie has one of the greatest plot twists you've ever encountered?

3. How would you describe the big turn or "twist" that takes place in our session in Esther today?

4. Are there some elements of today's story in Esther that you didn't see coming?

5. Who in your life is a valued source of the kind of difficult information you need to hear?

_____
_____
_____
_____

6. Why did Haman assume he would be the one the king wished to honor?

_____
_____
_____
_____

7. Why might the same king who had signed off on a decree to kill all the Jews now decide to honor a Jew so lavishly?

_____
_____
_____
_____

8. What stands out to you as an obvious lesson (or two) that we should take away from today's session in Esther?

_____
_____
_____
_____

9. Why should what almost happened to the Jews in this story so long ago matter to us today?

10. Have you pondered lately how fast life can change? What is one thing in life that has caught you off guard in the last year?

Session

Esther Exposes Haman

Focal text: Esther 7:1-10

Preoccupation

Have you ever arrived at a destination without any idea of how you drove there? As I write this, a friend recently posted a photo of her feet on social media. Both shoes were flats, but one was navy blue and the other was brown. She went to her office, to an appointment, and then to the grocery store and back home before she looked down that afternoon. Finally, she noticed how different her shoes truly were.

Can you imagine how preoccupied Haman was as he headed toward the banquet with King Ahasuerus and Queen Esther? That must have been one long walk for Haman, escorted by the eunuchs. Of course, considering Haman's character, there is every possibility that he stayed silent and used that time to search for a way out of the situation. If there was one power play left, he would find that option and use it to save himself. No doubt, he was pondering any possibilities.

How sobering might it have been, then, as he concluded that he was stuck? Haman was backed into a corner and left to suffer the results of his own legacy. Lavish food and drink have no taste when you are scared or in grief. Haman's meal was probably a distracted, ominous experience. Worse, this banquet went on and on. Notice in verse 2, on the second day of the banquet, the king finally asks Esther what she requests of him.

In sharp contrast to the urgency that must have been in Haman's soul, Esther is supremely cool. Possibly she knows now that she has the upper hand. Surely she has heard about Mordecai's honor (see Esth 6). Her cousin has been given his due and proclaimed a lofty person within the town square. With that, Haman will have to back off. He is now outflanked by Esther and Mordecai, whose unified importance has elevated their status with the king.

The Non-anxious Presence

Notice Esther's patience in carrying out her plan. Would you not want to blurt out your request the minute the king sat down with you? But on the second day of this banquet, the king has been charmed by Esther's presence. She has taken an extended chance to court him all over again. This is a happy king who, the text hints, has also been served a lot of wine by this point. Esther is marinating him for just the right moment.

Carol Bechtel says that the tone of this second banquet in chapter 7 appears to bend toward "drinking" rather than eating (62). In verse 1, the Hebrew word normally used for "banquet" is not used. Instead, the word *satah* is used, and it more often indicates alcohol or drink (Queen-Sutherland, 375–76). The NRSV renders the word "feast" rather than "banquet." Then, verse 2 refers to how much they have been "drinking wine," substantiating the word choice in verse 1.

Again, the writer refers to Esther as "Queen Esther," using her formal title. Her role and significance are growing in front of our eyes. This title also further foreshadows what is about to happen to Haman. The reader might sense that Haman's stature is shrinking as Esther's rises. Kandy Queen-Sutherland suggests that there is even more happening here. She points out that in contrast to earlier chapters, absent in chapter 7 is mention of the setting, décor, or lavishness. These kinds of details are so unimportant now that we do not know for certain where this feast occurs.

The focus is on the action rather than the setting. No longer are the king and Haman the only ones with power. Queen Esther is rising to her moment. As Queen-Sutherland points out, Esther's action has been wisely delayed. She is patiently preparing the king for her agenda, using the two days to test what her limits might be. How far can she go, and how fast? She will be disciplined enough to wait until the right moment, if the king gives her one.

Now in verse 2, her opportunity arrives. Twice in this verse, the king asks her what she wants. He says that she may have whatever it is. "What is your petition, Queen Esther? It shall be granted you. And what is your request? Even to the half of my kingdom, it shall be fulfilled." You may recall that this is the third time the king has begged her to make her request. Before, Esther was patient enough not to respond.

Finally, we see a strategic Esther seize her moment. Queen-Sutherland notes that Esther twice uses the title "king" in her request of Ahasuerus in verse 3. She wants to be sure he hears her recognizing his power and presence. Further, she couches her request in hope—"*If* I have won your favor . . . and *if* it pleases the king."

Her request also reflects a key aspect of her story. Esther asks for a twofold gift: "let my life be given me—that is my petition—and the lives of my people—that is my request" (v. 3). We easily relate to the first part. Even though she is a queen, her people are to be eliminated. Esther is not guaranteed to be saved from that edict once it is carried out. She is requesting that the king will grant her a reprieve for her own life. I would have done the same.

At a previous church, I served in a Baptist-Jewish dialogue group for years. We worked patiently, slowly even, to understand one another. In their honesty, many on the Jewish side of the group confided that they thought of themselves primarily as a "people" and less often as a religious entity. We Christians tend to think of the Jews as the root bed of our Judeo-Christian faith. Like my modern-day Jewish friends, Esther was also asking the king for the survival of a *people*.

As a canonical piece, Esther is one of two Old Testament books (the other being Ezra) set within a Persian context. Queen-Sutherland points out that these books share some themes, such as "exile." However, while Ezra appears to struggle with exiles in a Jewish setting, Esther is the Jewish exile struggling to survive in a foreign setting. We hear that struggle voiced honestly here as Esther explains her plea.

Anderson points out a compelling piece of verbiage. In verse 4, Esther elaborates on her people's story. "For we have been sold, I and my people, to be destroyed, to be killed, and to be annihilated. If we had been sold merely as slaves, men and women, I would have held my peace; but no enemy can compensate for this damage to the king." Three verbs here are important: "destroyed . . . killed . . . annihilated." These are dire circumstances, summing up what she sees as the result of the Jews being taken into the Persian Empire against their will.

However, how they got there is where Esther connects with her king. The phrase "we have been sold" employs a Hebrew word, *makar*, that often gets rendered "to sell," but Anderson believes it conveys a notion of "being turned over to one's enemies" (861). He cites its frequent use in the Old Testament book of Judges to make his case. In Judges, the notion of betrayal or sale to enemies is indicated each time *makar* is used there.

The Turn

Drunk though he may be, such strong imagery from his queen softens Ahasuerus. If a door swings on a hinge, then verse 5 is the hinge where the door of revelation swings open. The entire story of Esther moves in a new direction here as the king asks, "Who is he, and where is he, who has presumed to do this?" Imagine Esther perhaps raising an arm and pointing as in verse 6 she responds, "A foe and enemy! This wicked Haman!"

Read what happens next in verses 6b-7 and let it sit in your mind for a minute. Take in the irony.

> Then Haman was terrified before the king and the queen. The king rose from the feast in wrath and went into the palace garden, but Haman stayed to beg his life from Queen Esther, for he saw that the king had determined to destroy him.

In baseball, when someone is hit by a pitch or otherwise injured, the custom is to grant them a chance to "walk off" the pain. We know that emotionally, sometimes our response to great pain or shock is to first walk away, letting words or actions emerge later. Here, the king is caught between the queen and his trusted assistant. He grasps what has happened in a moment of clarity. Now, he needs a moment to let his mind catch up with his anger.

There are two obvious, parallel awakenings occurring here. The obvious one is that Esther is emerging as a truer queen. Also, for the first time her ethnicity is revealed to the king. Esther is rising, and now she is more fully known. However, the king is also awakening to the corrupt and damaging presence he has ushered into power in Haman. There will be more questions to ask and more for him to realize, but the fuller picture is coming into focus now.

Carol Bechtel urges fairness to the king at one subtle point. Perhaps the king misheard Haman back when he originally asked to "destroy" Esther's people. Bechtel contends that orally, the word "to sell" (*'ābad*) was nearly the same as "to destroy" (*'ābad*) (Bechtel, 64). Maybe the king thought Haman was asking permission to sell the Jewish people into slavery within their empire. While of course we will still object to such evil, this was apparently an option in their cultural place and time. In writing, though, the edict is clear that Haman's order was to destroy or kill the Jews. Now, in chapter 7, the king understands more clearly.

Surely This Can't Get Any Worse

What could possibly make this situation worse for Haman? The next two verses will show us. First, verse 8 offers an almost comical narrative—that is, if you dislike obvious villains and have viewed Haman in that role from the beginning of Esther. In Persian culture, it is likely that at such a feast the queen would recline on something referred to here as a "couch," or even a "bed" in some translations. Nothing in our text suggests that Haman intends a sexual act. In sheer terror (v. 6), he is begging for his life.

However, the king walks in from getting a breath of air just in time to see Haman. Haman is probably on his knees and perhaps clutching Queen Esther's feet or ankles. The text can also be read in a way that suggests he was on the couch with her. This would not have been an uncommon position for one who was begging.

The 2008 movie *Vantage Point* explored a political assassination in Spain. It showed the crime and the aftermath from about six different people's views or vantage points. Each time the shooting was replayed, a new detail emerged or a new understanding came to light. Drink in the irony of the mighty Haman, now pleading for his life from a woman. Of course, King Ahasuerus's interpretation of what he sees from a different angle is all that matters. He sees a crooked bully, now daring to assault his queen, and demands to know, "Will he even assault the queen in my presence, in my own house?"

Let's be sure to notice what is *not* in the text. What is silent, or missing, is any response from Esther. She could have spoken for or against Haman further. She could have at least cleared up what the king thinks he is seeing. Haman is pleading for his life. Instead of explaining to the king, Esther sits silently, knowing that she has done her work. Sometimes in life, we, like Haman, are left to face the consequences of our misdeeds.

Scholars debate the inspiration for what "covered Haman's face" in verse 8. Some believe that a covered face in ancient Greek and Roman culture was a sign of capital punishment to come. We might interpret that the king was damning Haman to be executed as he spoke. However, no one has substantiated this practice or symbolism in the Persian culture of the time. A more Hebrew understanding might be that Haman covered his own face in reaction to what the king said.

Making Haman's situation worse is a silent, humble servant who finally speaks up. My mother once worked as a bookkeeper for a wealthy man. She saw a cavalcade of beautiful women and powerful men come through, each with their own set of wants from this rich man. They took advantage of his weaknesses and often manipulated him blatantly. Because of where she worked, my mother sometimes knew most parts of the story. However, she has told me many times that key pieces of information only came her way once the maid whispered details to her. Often, the seemingly behind-the-scenes workers are privy to the most personal information.

Harbona is one of the eunuchs serving the king in verse 9. Like the maid in my mother's workplace, the eunuch's job was to serve and to remain otherwise silent and even unseen. Thus, the eunuchs saw and knew things that not everyone else was privy to. Harbona speaks up now and points out to the king that Haman has a means of execution at the ready. It had been intended for Mordecai. Conveniently, this newly built gallows was at Haman's own house, standing fifty cubits high. Characteristic of all we have read in Esther, Ahasuerus takes the bait and announces his new plan. Haman is to be hanged, apparently quite soon (v. 10).

You will have to work out how you feel about the capital punishment bestowed on Haman. As the book of Esther has made evident, this kind of punishment was a common option in that time and place. That is not for us to change, or to like or dislike. It is simply where this chapter ends. As with all our sessions thus far, you will also have to work to apply what we are reading to your life of faith. Does good win out over evil? Finally, in this chapter, it appears that it does. Can people awaken and maybe even change themselves? Ahasuerus might have. Esther might be living into a bold new realm as well. Is life lived in chapters? Yes, and perhaps a new one has begun for a few of our characters here.

1. What is the most preoccupied you have ever felt? Why?

_____
_____
_____
_____
_____

2. Have you ever arrived somewhere, but looking back you don't even recall how you got yourself there?

_____
_____
_____
_____
_____

3. What do you think Haman was thinking about on his long walk to the queen's banquet at the beginning of our story today?

_____
_____
_____
_____
_____

4. How would you sum up Esther's strategy?

_____
_____
_____
_____

5. Why do you think she took this particular approach to the problem?

_____
_____
_____
_____

6. What is the most patient you've ever had to be, awaiting the right chance to deal with a problem? What did you learn from this experience?

_____
_____
_____
_____
_____

7. In today's story, how do we see Esther's role and significance growing right before us?

_____
_____
_____
_____
_____

8. How do previously minor figures in the overall Esther story emerge as quite large in today's session?

_____
_____
_____
_____
_____

9. What comment or perspective might the larger biblical account offer on how Haman's gallows prepared for another is now to be used against him in his own execution?

_____
_____
_____
_____
_____

10. How do you deal with the capital punishment as depicted in today's story? If the thought of someone being punished by death is appalling, how can you still learn from our story?

_____
_____
_____
_____
_____

Session 8

Esther and Mordecai Are Rewarded

Focal text: Esther 8:1-8

Have We Learned Anything?

Have we learned anything yet from these stories? We might pose that question to King Ahasuerus if we could talk with him. As soon as Haman is dead, we see the king give Esther the house that once belonged to Haman. Then the king gives his signet ring to Mordecai. We will come back to the implications of these drastic actions. Ultimately, we are the only ones who get the chance to learn this story's lessons, for we get to participate as citizens informed by stories like this one. The king appears to readily hand off his power and blessing this time to these characters. While we may be biased to believe they will handle that responsibility better than Haman did, this can feel like Ahasuerus readying himself to slip back into a slumber. Inattention on his part allowed the Esther story to unfold as it did. Do we want inattentive leaders? Do we approve of such ultimate power being concentrated in one person's hands, as in Haman's case?

One of our challenges any time we open the ancient Scripture is to ask ourselves, "What am I supposed to learn from this?" It would be too easy to dismiss the book of Esther as a fascinating story from a different time and place. Perhaps a voice inside you says, "I am not a king or a queen. I don't have a palace or an empire. There's nothing much for me here."

Contrary to many people's view of the Bible, I would challenge you to consider that not every verse of Scripture is a command or an imperative for your life. Some of Scripture is best viewed as a cautionary tale—or an inspiring one—rather than as a verse-by-verse playbook for how to live. Some texts ought to instruct our living and we should follow them. Part of the responsibility believers carry as students of the Bible is to bring discernment to how we debrief the sacred word.

At this point in the larger Esther story, what do you feel you have taken away or learned? Esther challenges us to be either wiser, bolder, or more principled. Esther cautions us about the excesses that could come with our positions. Esther warns us about devaluing any segment of humanity, including the unwanted or outcast people groups in our own cities. Maybe Esther has reminded you of the dangerous potential of injustice or that you need to pay more attention to a specific contemporary issue.

Just Rewards

If we have found ourselves rooting for Esther and Mordecai, this is the chapter where we smile on their behalf. We can finally exhale. Things are being set in order, and our heroes are safe. In fact, they are rewarded. They have earned this.

Reidar B. Bjornard says, "It was quite according to the practices of the ancient Near East that a winner took over the property of a loser, so the king gave Haman's house to Esther" (16). Bernard Anderson confirms in his notes that the state would have had power to confiscate the property of convicted criminals such as Haman (864).

But don't relax yet. Our heroes may be safe at this point in the story, but their larger people group is still under the death decree. The previous order, sealed with the king's own signet ring under Haman, still applies. There is still a date by which all Jews are to be rounded up and readied for execution. An order from the king is irrevocable except by the king himself.

Now in chapter 8, the king knows just about everything he has previously ignored. He has called Mordecai in to be honored yet again. Let's look for a moment at what King Ahasuerus has given to Esther and to Mordecai. In Esther 5:11, Haman gathered his wife and friends together apparently just so he could remind them how wealthy and powerful he was. When the king gives Haman's house to Esther, she turns around and passes it to Mordecai (v. 2).

Recall that earlier, in Esther 3:9, Haman had sweetened the deal to kill the Jews with a gift of 10,000 talents of silver. This was a gift to the king, basically a fee to get permission to kill the Jews. A "talent" was an ancient unit of measure. Used to calculate wealth, it could apply either to gold or silver. One talent weighed roughly 33–35 kilograms or 75 pounds.

Think of how much silver it would take to weigh 75 pounds! One talent was worth approximately 6,000 drachmas or denarii, and a single drachma or denarius was considered to be one day's wage. Attempts to convert an ancient biblical "silver talent" to an approximate US dollar amount today would fascinate us but would likely be off-base. At that time, silver was worth relatively more than it is worth today. Suffice it to say, 10,000 talents added up to a lot of money in the ancient world. Haman was doing quite well financially when his punishment came down.

If Haman could afford that much to pay for permission to assuage a grudge, then one might suppose he had plenty of wealth left afterward. One's "house" came along with everything else they had, including all other wealth. But what would a queen do with such a house or all that wealth when she already lived in a palace with a king?

What would happen to Haman's wife, Zeresh, after Haman's execution? Kandy Queen-Sutherland points out that the story is not concerned with sympathy for those who depended on Haman. In this ancient part of the world, Zeresh's fortunes as a woman were attached to Haman's well-being (Queen-Sutherland, 418). The same applied to his sons. They were seen partly as labor, partly as heirs, and partly as property. Even sons were viewed as an indicator of how prominent and blessed their father had become. That is likely why the sons were mentioned when Haman celebrated his wealth and status.

In 8:3, we see that Esther is not yet ready to celebrate. Rather, she effectively starts over in her approach to the king. If we think she has risen to full power, verses 3-4 remind us that there is still a vast distance between her and the king. Remember from chapter 5, she must not make a request of the king without being invited to do so.

Are her tears genuine in verse 3? When we consider the context, there is no reason to think they are not. Queen-Sutherland believes the Hebrew text evokes the truth of Esther's emotion. The word *hithannen* is a combination of two words, *weeping* and *pleading*, in our current English (Queen-Sutherland, 424). This is the countenance and posture of a woman in desperation. Her people's lives are still on the line. Her posture should grip our attention as we read what happens next.

His anger having passed with Haman's execution, the king extends the golden scepter and invites Esther to make the request (v. 4). As if we aren't convinced of Esther's humble posture and practice, verses 5 and 6 record the careful, almost formulaic wording of her request:

> "If it pleases the king, and if I have won his favor, and if the thing seems right before the king, and I have his approval, let an order be written to revoke the letters devised by Haman son of Hammedatha the Agagite, which he wrote giving orders to destroy the Jews who are in all the provinces of the king. For how can I bear to see the calamity that is coming on my people? Or how can I bear to see the destruction of my kindred?"

Notice the three-fold beginning, "If it pleases . . . if I have won . . . if the thing seems right . . . ." We learn well from Esther if she reminds us that even in our bravery, we may still have strictures to follow. That is common in our lives. Esther is exercising her power. She is on the edge of accomplishing what truly matters. However, she still is not in charge, and protocols are still in place.

Next, she gets to the serious business of asking the king to revoke the standing order that is still in danger of being carried out. In our current world of instant communication, we can forget that there was a time when circulating an announcement or an order was a daunting task. Trying to rescind or change that order required the same laborious process.

Verse 6 sums up Esther's true mission in two questions: "For how can I bear to see the calamity that is coming on my people? Or how can I bear to see the destruction of my kindred?" If timing is an important element in life, Esther's request here is punctuated by this personal note. The king is a sympathetic audience. Perhaps for the first time, he sees the Jews as more than just another people group among his empire's holdings. They now have a face and a name in his queen and in the man who saved his life. It could be that they are of value to him as humans for the first time.

Read verses 7-8 aloud. How do you react to Ahasuerus's response? Do you find what he says here somehow both satisfying and conflicting? On the one hand, we exhale as readers. Esther's true business has been stated. The king has received it well and takes decisive action. The Jews will be spared. Esther and Mordecai are free to write a retraction of the order and circulate it with the king's seal set upon it.

On the other hand, we may feel as though the king has learned little. He has not reformed his ways because he quickly turns great power over to Esther and Mordecai to write up the order. It is like Mordecai is the new Haman. Perhaps we should remember that even in the ancient world, the business of running a vast empire was complex. A monarch would have relied on empowered assistants like Haman and now Mordecai.

Sadly, though, it seems like Ahasuerus wants to retreat to his inattentive ways as quickly as possible. He may not want to be bothered with running a kingdom. As readers, we will not get to solve that issue in this story. We will have to accept King Ahasuerus as he is portrayed. Admit, though, that you may like this new arrangement. We like Esther and we like Mordecai. With Esther's counsel, it appears that the wise Mordecai has risen to sit at the controls. If you are like me, you feel more comfortable with that end to the story because you trust them.

When you are living through something one day at a time, the experience simply looks like life. The essence of a story can elude us if it's told one chapter at a time. Let's look back now over the larger picture of Esther. Charles Dorothy has collected what he calls in this story "a series of reversals." They have been on display for us since Esther's story began, one movement at a time:
• Haman is forced to honor Mordecai, 6:6-12
• Haman's doom is assured by the same wife and friends who advised him to kill Mordecai earlier, 6:13
• Esther exposes Haman for what he is, 7:5-6
• Haman is executed, 7:9-10
• Esther is given Haman's estate; Mordecai is given the ring of power and replaces Haman, 8:1-2
• Esther begs Ahasuerus to overturn the impending evil of Haman's edict, 8:3-6
• A second edict is granted that reverses the first edict, 8:3-14

Life is full of surprises, and so is God. God is at work in this story, even if the Divine is not directly named. And now we have one more reversal to go. That will come in the next session. After that, we have some celebrating to do.

1. How do you react to the way the king rewards Mordecai and Esther? Does any aspect alarm you?

2. To this point in the story of Esther, what are two or three lessons we should be learning?

3. What are some aspects of the Esther story that should be timeless and instructive for us in our current era?

4. Why did the king give Esther the house and belongings of Haman? What made that a normal occurrence in their day?

5. Why couldn't Esther bring herself to celebrate just yet?

6. How could Esther and Mordecai be safe while their people were still in danger?

7. Read verses 7-8 aloud. How do you react to Ahasuerus's response here? Do you find what he says somehow both satisfying and conflicting?

8. What further request does Esther make of the king? Why is this necessary?

9. See above Charles Dorothy's list of "reversals" portrayed in the book of Esther. What lessons about God do these reversals have for us? What lessons about humanity?

_____
_____
_____
_____
_____

10. What will you take away from studying this session that might help you grow as a person? What about it might mature your faith?

_____
_____
_____
_____
_____

Session 9

Rescue of the Jews

Focal text: Esther 8:9-17

How Momentum Nearly Caused a Genocide Anyway

You think the story ended last week, don't you? Everything's okay now. You've already exhaled. But maybe you did that a little too soon. We've still got work to do in our story. As our text for this session begins, the Jewish people throughout the empire are still in danger.

Momentum was one of the more memorable and helpful concepts I recall studying in basic high school science. This notion holds that once an object is set in motion, that object will continue in its path even after its energy or propulsion has been ceased—at least until something changes its power or its stored-up power is exhausted. For instance, a car that has begun to roll forward can have its engine turned off, yet it may continue to roll forward for a time. Its sheer weight will keep it moving forward until it runs out of stored-up energy or at least until its gearing, its brakes, or an obstacle causes it to stop.

Our big orange cat tries to chase his smaller sister at times. He'll reach his top speed only to see her make a sudden cut into another room. If he's on a hardwood floor, he may try his best to turn. But occasionally he skids out of control because his hulking body has momentum that continues to move him forward. In World War II, the May 1945 celebration of allied victory in Europe marked the end of conflict for many. Because you don't turn off a massive war by signing a surrender agreement, a bitter insurgency in Germany fought the Allied troops for months. Momentum took the war forward for a time.

Earlier in chapter 8, King Ahasuerus saw things Esther's way. Haman was hanged on his own personal gallows. The king elevated

Mordecai to Haman's vacated spot as his second in command. Esther received the gift of Haman's estate. The king declared that all the Jews should be spared.

This is great except for the momentum that is still at work in the story. This is unthinkable in a digital, instant world like today, but getting word around in that time was difficult. Undoing something that you had set in motion weeks ago took a lot of effort. As verse 9 begins, there is a race against time. Throughout the empire, the order for the Jews to be killed remains in effect, with the king's own signet ring as its seal.

Sivan is the third month of the Jewish or Hebrew calendar that is still in use by some today. It is lunar based, and it originally captured much of the agricultural rhythm of ancient Hebrew life. Over the centuries, there have been some basic changes to the Jewish calendar, but its import stands due to the ties to significant moments or celebrations in Jewish tradition.

Sivan lasts roughly thirty days and overlaps parts of what we know as May and June in our Gregorian calendar. Also in Jewish history, Moses is said to have received the Torah at Mount Sinai in the month of Sivan. King David was both born and later died in the month of Sivan. Even today, what happens in this session is also a high mark on the Jewish calendar for the month of Sivan. On the twenty-third day, Mordecai wrote an edict that undid Haman's previous one.

Not an Email, Text Message, or Social Media Account in the Bunch

The challenge now is to get the new edict circulated quickly and thoroughly enough to halt the massacre of the Jews. Verses 9-14 capture the massive effort this required. Read through the text again and count all the steps involved to publicize the new order.

Governments, militaries, and large companies can get word around instantly these days. Plans can seemingly spin on a dime because of instant communication. Networks, groups, teams, and entire employee rosters can be sent the same information in a matter of seconds. Location across the world is not a factor. This was obviously not the case in Esther's day.

When big news breaks today, think about how it circulates. We still live in a transitional age where news is concerned. An announcement is made at a press conference. There are still traditional news agencies, fragile though they may be, that weren't even a dream in

Esther's time. A press release may go out electronically; online news organizations and broadcast television news often begin the circulation of a news story. Then social media kicks in by distributing these published or released stories.

Where we live currently, a local business made big news not long ago. They were leasing a major new space in our city and investing tremendous amounts of money. New jobs would be created and their operations expanded. We heard ahead of time that a local company had big economic news to break, but no one knew what company until the announcement was made. I was in Slovakia on the day the big news was scheduled to break.

Meanwhile, my wife was at her job in our city. The announcement was made at the appointed time, and I got word while sitting in a traffic jam along the Slovakian/Hungarian border. I relayed it to her immediately. Late that afternoon, she encountered the family who owns the company that was expanding. She congratulated them. They asked her how she knew already. She replied, "Oh, my husband is over in Slovakia and he heard. He told me." They laughed, thinking she would have heard the news from someone who was currently in town.

All of King Ahasuerus's secretaries drafted the decree according to what Mordecai dictated. A "satrap" was a governor set over a province within the ancient Persian Empire. Apparently, there was another layer of leaders simply referred to as "governors." Then other officials in every province were included in the communication chain. Also, perhaps, the leaders of Jewish bodies within the empire were notified (see v. 9).

The amount of detail in this chapter of Esther is helpful. At that time, the king was trying to communicate with 127 provinces. Not everyone wrote in the same way because not everyone spoke the same language. As an example, the kingdom is said to stretch "from India to Ethiopia" in verse 9. Letters had to be written in many diverse ways so that every recipient could read them and understand the new edict.

Little Time to Spare

Now we find out how little time there was to circulate this word. Mordecai's decree was recorded and then sealed with the king's ring so that it carried the full weight of the palace. Horse-bound couriers set off in every direction, racing to see that the new orders were received in the quickest way possible. These royal steeds would have made quite the entrance into any city, their royal riders distinctive and well known. Though foreign to us today, mustering of the court's vast resources this way spread a unified word across the empire faster than anyone else could have done. In its time, this dissemination of news was state of the art and aggressive.

It seems that the thirteenth day of the month of Adar was the appointed day when all Jews were to be annihilated across the Persian Empire (v. 12). At first reading, then, we might wonder what all the fuss was about. If we're in Sivan, the third month, and none of this will happen until Adar, the twelfth month, then why the hurry? Again, word spread slowly and with uncertainty in a day when there was no way to duplicate, print, or otherwise mass-produce documents. They wanted to allow all the time possible for the actual person-to-person broadcast of this new order. That could take months and months.

Another practical matter would require some time. Beginning in verse 11, we see a detailed and specific set of instructions to the Jewish people. On that one day, previously scheduled for their demise, they will be allowed to defend themselves. They can assemble and form troops to fight against the armed forces of any city or province that might attack them. This kind of action did not happen overnight. Their salvation, and their empowerment, was to be announced in every city and province by public decree. How serious was the Jewish protection in this decree? Look at verse 11, which seems to permit them even to plunder the goods of any attacking force that should come up against them on that day. That was an accepted practice of military victory at the time. It was not an open-ended arrangement. But for one day, the Jews had comprehensive empowerment.

In one congregation I served, a woman contacted me at the office. I had recently visited her mother in a local nursing home. She wanted to thank me for going by periodically to do so. She had an interesting request. "Obviously, I hope you'll continue to see Mom every now and then." I assured her I would. "Oh, and one other thing—would you be sure you do what you've been doing and leave a business card each time?" I assumed this was so she would know when I had been by. "No," she said, and then explained, "Every time the staff see you walk down the hall and into her room, my mother looks more important to them. Someone besides me cares enough about her that they are looking in on her. Every time they see your business card there on her side table, they'll also know you've been there. It makes her 'somebody' in a world where you could become nobody awfully quick."

Suddenly in Esther, a small and marginalized people group were receiving quite the spotlight. A peripheral benefit would come far after the thirteenth of Adar. Let's even bet that there were parts within the vast empire where some people had not even heard of the Jews. That changed now. The Jews mattered. They had the imperial protection of no less than the king.

Some things changed as a result of this attention and the importance the Jews had taken on. Did you notice this as our story wound down? Verses 15-17 rattle off a joyful list of things that should strike us as positive. Mordecai is festooned in regal colors and fine robes, signaling an important turn of fate for him. If we like it when the "good guy" wins, we are glad that Mordecai is now safe and in a position of reward. Even better, the people seem to be in more responsible hands. The Jews, once on the brink of extinction, now have "light" and "gladness" (v. 16). When was the last time that seemed to be the case for them? The very last verse seems to imply that people who aren't Jews have begun to identify as Jewish (v. 17). That is shocking. How far they have come!

1. What is your understanding of how "momentum" works?

2. What is the best example you can think of where you have experienced momentum in real life?

3. When big corporate or national news breaks today, what are some specific ways that news circulates?

4. If you lived 2,500 years ago, what might you need to communicate an urgent, time-sensitive message to every person and village in a vast empire consisting of multiple nations and ethnicities?

5. What are some specific steps you might need to take to get your message out?

_____
_____
_____
_____

6. With seemingly a few months to spare, why did Mordecai hurry convey the message that would give the Jews the right to defend themselves?

_____
_____
_____
_____

7. Other than being saved from genocide, what benefit did the Jews get within the empire once this decree went forth?

_____
_____
_____
_____

8. What level of danger do you perceive the Jews still faced, now that the king's new decree had gone out?

_____
_____
_____
_____

9. What lesson has this session taught you?

_____
_____
_____
_____
_____

10. How does what we've studied in this session apply to the world in which you live today?

_____
_____
_____
_____
_____

Establishment of Purim and Aftermath

Session 10

Focal text: Esther 9–10

To finish our study of the book of Esther, we have chapters 9 and 10. Don't worry—you may have already discovered that this is not as much reading as it seems. Chapter 10, particularly, consists of only one paragraph. Importantly, the aftermath of all the previous action is resolved in a fitting tribute. The establishment of the Feast of Purim was a way of memorializing this dangerous moment in Jewish history.

In an episode of the Netflix show *Somebody Feed Phil*, Phil Rosenthal prepares to enjoy a feast. Best known as the writer and producer of the long-running sitcom *Everybody Loves Raymond*, in these episodes Rosenthal leads viewers on an enjoyable global romp disguised as a culinary tour. He is open about his Jewish roots and occasionally pokes fun at his heritage. At one meal, he proclaims, "Our whole history consists of 'Somebody tried to kill us all . . . they didn't succeed . . . let's eat!'"

We'll get to the feast in a bit. To this day, Purim commemorates the events portrayed in Esther and is observed annually by Jews the world over. We discussed the power and occasional dangers of *momentum* in the last session, and we will certainly see it in action during this study.

A Day of Reckoning

As Esther 9 begins, the thirteenth day of the twelfth month, the month of Adar, has arrived. This is the day on which the annihilation of the Jews was to have taken place, if not for King Ahasuerus's new decree. Mordecai is wise enough to know that some may not hear of the changed order. There may even be people who wish to wipe out the Jews badly enough to attack them anyway. The new order, then, provides for a day of defense: the thirteenth day of Adar. The Jews can, without fear of retribution, defend themselves should anyone proceed to attack them on that day.

When have you ever seen someone rise to great power after humble beginnings? Does a historic figure come to mind? What did they do with that newfound power?

Notice how quickly things can turn, as "the fear of Mordecai" is attributed to the developments here. Esther 9:1-10 chronicles the action. Some skirmishes break out. Additionally, the Jews seem to attack the sons of Haman. We do not know who attacked whom first; the sons may have banded together an army. Scholars note that history does not record, outside the Bible, any violence in this place and time that would match this story in Esther.

Also noteworthy is the detail that "they did not touch the plunder" in verse 10. The new order that Mordecai had written specifically allowed Jews to plunder the goods of anyone who may have taken up arms against them. If victorious, they were entitled to the spoils of war on this one special day. That was a commonly accepted practice of the time. Why might the Jews have been careful, then, to pass up that gain?

The description of the first day's action is brief. However, what becomes clear is that the day was bloody in certain localities. It was also decisive. The passage of time had given the Jews a chance to be armed and ready, even though there was no certainty that they would be attacked. They were attacked, though, and they defended themselves as provided for in Mordecai's decree.

Verses 11-15 give the impression that all was not yet settled, at least in Susa. Notice that for the fourth time in the book of Esther, King Ahasuerus asks Esther what her request is. But this is the first time that he does not make any drastic or lavish promises along with his question. He simply asks her what more she wants (Queen-Sutherland, 462). Each time before, he has promised her up to half of his kingdom. Now, perhaps because he is finally sober, he only wants information.

What Does Esther Want?

Esther does in fact want something more. Her request is that the king will grant an extra day for fighting. Has Esther become a killer? Has a seemingly meek, cautious person become an aggressive and bloodthirsty warrior? Perhaps she and Mordecai have heard of further threats. Maybe they know of more people who would like to attack the Jews and recognize that until these threats are neutralized, they will never truly be safe.

Queen-Sutherland, in particular, points out that there is an "inter-textual" reality between Esther 9 and 1 Samuel 15 (459–61). In 1 Samuel, the strife between the Jews and the Amalekites is explained. King Saul and the Jews attack King Agag and the Amalekites. Apparently, these two groups had fought since the exodus from Egypt. Not following God's instructions to eradicate the Amalekites from the land, Saul instead took some of their things but left many of the people living there. He also spared King Agag's life.

No matter how we may feel about God's instructions in that passage, it is the way the ancient story reads. In 1 Samuel, the prophet Samuel follows up on this battle with King Saul and points out his disobedience to God. As a consequence, King Saul will be rejected by God as king of Israel. Whether a documented point of history or simply a story repeated in Jewish lore, this conflict is the source of animosity between the Jews and the Amalekites. You may remember that early on, the book of Esther establishes Haman as an "Agagite" (3:1).

Now in Esther, Haman's descendants are still an issue. On the thirteenth day, this first day of battle, the ten sons of Haman have been defeated and killed. Esther (perhaps in league with Mordecai) wants to make a public statement. The Jews are to be accepted and should be attacked only at one's own peril. She asks permission to hang the ten sons of Haman from the gallows. They will be an example and may symbolize a decisive end to the Amalekite conflict that has raged for generations. We should remember here that Haman had the gallows built in order to make an example of Mordecai. This is another in the continuing series of surprising "turns" as a theme in Esther.

Why Didn't They Grab the Loot?

Again, for a third time in this chapter, it is reported that there was no plunder taken by the prevailing Jews (see vv. 10, 15, 16). Queen-Sutherland poses the notion that this might further symbolize the finality of the victory in the Jews' long-running conflict with the Amalekites. When might you not take someone's plunder, even though you could? When the enemy is so decisively beaten that they are no longer important.

We will see for a third time in this ninth chapter the same notation. They did not take the plunder. Some believe this may symbolize a turning back of King Saul's original decision, as 1 Samuel 15:24b documents him only taking part of the plunder after war with the Amalekites because he still feared them. With this pattern of not taking plunder, a signal is sent. You might subscribe to the notion that the opposite of love is not hate but rather indifference. Here, the Jews are indifferent to the Amalekites' belongings. There will be no more fear now. The Amalekite tension is over. Their possessions are not even worthy of being possessed by the victors.

The literal number given for the human loss of life is steep (see 9:12, 16). While we have paid attention to the Amalekite issues that date back for many years, they were likely not the only people with ill will toward the Jews. We do not know exactly who tried to attack these newly empowered Jews during the two days of fighting. In all, some 75,000 lost their lives in skirmishes outside Susa (v. 16). This was a decisive and unmistakable statement across the empire. The Jews were an important part of Persia, and they were protected for the foreseeable future.

The Feast of Purim Established

In Esther 9:18-32, a new commemoration is set forth. As was the Jewish custom, the people marked this victorious and relieving outcome with the establishment of a feast. From this need to celebrate came the Feast of Purim.

Can you imagine the quiet and peace that may finally have been afforded to Esther, Mordecai, and their people? This notion of a day of rest that they enjoyed on the fifteenth of the month is a fitting observance. An ethnic group breathed a collective sigh of relief. Although God is not specifically mentioned as the receiver of their gratitude, people of faith may choose to infer that they raised their collective thanks to the Divine One.

Let's consider the meaning of the word *Purim*. Mordecai "enjoined" the Jews (v. 21); in other words, he "instructed or encouraged them" to keep this yearly feast with a written decree. Yet there is an important distinction. Purim is regarded as a traditional practice but not a "law" within Judaism. The root of the word is "Pur," which is said to have a non-Jewish origin. That word means "lot," as in the random drawing system some used to solve problems. The biblical writer even explains this in verse 24. As many Jewish commemorations do, this Feast of Purim has a second name. It is sometimes called the "Festival of Lots" (Rylaarsdam, 968).

What Haman had decreed about the Jewish annihilation was regarded as a terrible draw of the lot. Maybe there was no explanation for what Haman wished to do, so the randomness of his decision to kill the Jews was described as a "lot" that they as a people had drawn. The dramatic reversal here in Esther undoes the intent of that lot. Purim, then, marks their salvation from a terrible fate or lot.

Mordecai's written instructions were specific. Because two days were involved in the crisis, depending on the region or town one lived in, the fourteenth and fifteenth days of Adar were to be set aside for the observance. The overall purpose was for celebration and remembrance. *Celebration* is an experience we understand well, and it is not always the same as *remembrance*. I hear older generations in America, for instance, make a distinction between the two. They will emphasize that holidays like Memorial Day or July Fourth are days of "remembrance," lest we forget the sacrifices made to keep our independence possible. While many of us travel on these days, or have a gathering and fire up the grill, there are many who lament that the remembrance aspect might get too little attention.

In that spirit, note the specific ways in which these days were to be used. During the feast of Purim, the Jews were to

- hold a feast and celebrate;
- give gifts of food to one another;
- feed the poor, that they too may be a part of the celebration;
- perhaps give other types of gifts to the poor;
- read the Scroll of Esther publicly so that all might hear the story again; and
- offer special prayers in gratitude.

You will notice in Esther 9 that these two days of celebration and remembrance were to be kept for time unending, perpetuated among the generations yet to come and across all Jewish people. In modern times, this feast is typically observed during either February or March, varying by the year. Despite the technicality that this feast was not established as "law," Esther 9 does imply that this celebration was institutionalized widely as a custom.

The balance of Esther gives a summary of all that has happened. Queen Esther herself gives "full written authority, confirming this second letter" (v. 29)—the second letter being the one in which Mordecai enjoined the Purim practice. Esther even calls this a "command" from the queen (v. 32). The practice has survived even to this day, with many Jews still observing Purim as a permanent part of their calendars. Queen-Sutherland makes an interesting observation about the close of Esther 9 and the three verses that compose chapter 10. That is, like the biblical book of Ruth, Esther ends with a glance into a future that lives beyond the days of fear, victory, and the first celebration of Purim.

Esther 10:1 establishes the vastness of King Ahasuerus's empire. It stretched from the land across to the islands of the sea. Then, in verse 2, we are assured that there is more to this story. Not all of the king's powerful acts are recorded, nor is the extent of the honor that was accorded to Mordecai written down. In verse 3, we end the book on a hopeful note. That is, Mordecai did not just rule with the great power afforded him. He ruled with compassion and goodness, keeping the welfare of the people at heart. Considering how Haman used his power, this may be some of the best news in the entire book of Esther. If you like a happy ending, this is a brief one, but it is certainly a good note on which to conclude our study.

1. One Jewish entertainer has said, "Our whole history consists of 'Somebody tried to kill us all . . . they didn't succeed . . . let's eat!'" Thinking about Scripture, history, and culture, why do you think this might be an apt statement?

_____
_____
_____
_____
_____

2. When have you seen someone rise to great power after humble beginnings? Does a historic figure come to mind?

_____
_____
_____
_____
_____

3. In the example you thought of, what did they do with that newfound power?

_____
_____
_____
_____
_____

4. If the accepted practice in war at that time was for the victor to plunder the spoils of the defeated, why might the Jews have declined to take any plunder on this day?

_____
_____
_____
_____
_____

5. What statement or symbol might they have communicated by declining what they could have taken?

_____
_____
_____
_____
_____

6. Thinking of the Feast of Purim, why might a day of relative rest be a fitting way to celebrate and remember?

_____
_____
_____
_____
_____

7. Why was the "Feast of Purim" also known as the "Feast of Lots"?

_____
_____
_____
_____
_____

8. In Esther 9–10, or in the larger Esther story, where are some places that you have seen God at work?

_____
_____
_____
_____
_____

9. What about your faith or heritage will look different to you because you have studied Esther?

___
___
___
___

10. Although God is not directly named in the book of Esther, where has God shown up within the Esther story?

___
___
___
___

Works Cited

Anderson, Bernhard W. *Kings, Chronicles, Ezra, Nehemiah, Esther, Job*. Volume 3 of Interpreter's Bible Commentary. New York: Abingdon, 1954.

Bechtel, Carol. *Esther*. Interpretation: A Bible Commentary for Teaching and Preaching. Louisville, KY: John Knox Press, 2002.

Bjornard, Reidar B. "Esther." In *Esther–Psalms*, volume 4 in The Broadman Bible Commentary. Nashville: Broadman, 1971.

Brontë, Charlotte. *Villette*. New York: Modern Library, 2001.

Dorothy, Charles V. *The Books of Esther: Structure, Genre and Textual Integrity*. JSOTSup187. Sheffield: Sheffield Academic Press, 1997.

Jacobs, Joseph, and Wilhelm Nowack. "Sackcloth." In the Jewish Encyclopedia online, 1906 version. jewishencyclopedia.com/articles/12981-sackcloth.

Johnson, James Weldon. "Vashti." In *Fifty Years & Other Poems, 1863–1913*. Boston: The Cornhill Company, c. 1917. gutenberg.org/ebooks/17884.

McCullough, W. S. "AHASUREUS." In *Encyclopædia Iranica* I/6 (1984/2011): 634–35. iranicaonline.org/articles/ahasureus.

Peters, Tom, and Robert H. Waterman. *In Search of Excellence*. New York: Harper and Row Publishers, 1982.

Queen-Sutherland, Kandy. *Ruth and Esther*. Smyth & Helwys Bible Commentary Series. Macon, GA: Smyth & Helwys Publishing, 2018.

Rylaarsdam, J. C. "*Purim.*" Interpreter's Dictionary of the Bible, volume K–Q. Nashville: Abingdon, 1962, 1984.

Stowe, Harriet Beecher. *Women in Sacred History: A Series of Sketches.* New York: J. B. Ford and Company, 1873. Available at archive.org/details/womaninsacredhis01stow/mode/2up.